How to be a Popular Crew

Everything you need to know to be welcomed on board again and again

Dave Robson

TSL Publications

Published in Great Britain in 2018
By TSL Publications, Rickmansworth

Copyright © 2018 Dave Robson
ISBN: 978-1-911070-89-4

Cover photo courtesy of pixabay.com

Dedications

To my beloved wife Rachella for sharing with me her love of the sea, and for being the very best crew a skipper could ask for.

To my late parents for imbuing in me a positive, can-do attitude, without which I would have given up years ago.

To the countless skippers and instructors who have given me, over the years, many priceless opportunities to learn how to crew and sail.

Last but by no means least, to the many wonderful people who have crewed with me and for me, and to those as yet unknown who will do so in the future.

INTRODUCTION

According to anecdotal evidence gathered from more than thirty three years of hanging around the sailing scene, it seems that only a tiny percentage of newcomers to sailing, people who aspire to crewing on yachts, get invited back to crew again, while the mystified majority are left on the quayside wondering what they did wrong or didn't do right.

For that reason I concluded that crew members who repeatedly get invited to come back to crew another day are members of a tiny elite.

The ideas, suggestions and true stories that follow attempt to dispel some of this mystique so you can join that elite – if you've got, or are willing to develop, the special qualities required of everyone who goes to sea.

My unabashed aim, via the information in this book, is to help you become the most sought-after crew person in your yacht club.

When I took up sailing after my divorce in 1984 I knew no one who sailed, let alone anyone who had a boat, but luckily some intuitive prompting from inside, you could call it wisdom from a higher place, guided me to make a start and to follow up virtually every opportunity that came my way – and there were many.

I don't really know what it was, but some inner drive or passion pushed me to get going on this path and from that, probably the first thing I learned was that when you follow your heart without hesitation and start taking appropriate action, opportunities always come your way. Incidentally, that applies to anything in your life, not just sailing, so it's a very useful realisation to take on board. But though I believe it is perfectly possible and realistic for anyone to live their dream, at the same time we have to be practical and acknowledge that it's easy to be put off.

If you want to learn to sail and get into yachting as an aspiring crew, or you are a new yacht club member wondering what planet skippers come from, what on earth they want from you, what you have to do to get invited on board and, most of all, how to get invited to come again, I hope this book will give you at least some of the support, insight, inside knowledge and guidance you need.

CONTENTS

CHAPTER ONE

WHAT'S IN A CREW?

"You can't get the crew these days."

This moan has been a familiar mantra in my yacht club ever since I can remember, even though we have a list of members, the majority of whom do not have their own boats but who desperately want to get afloat. And I gather the story is the same in many other yacht clubs throughout the land and beyond.

Not only that, but often I hear a body of the non-boat owning club members who see themselves as potential crew members complaining that they never or rarely seem to get to go out on other members' yachts. Why not? Because they don't get invited.

So we have the paradoxical situation where skippers are crying out for crew and going sailing short handed, while others who want to go sailing but don't have boats are left ashore. Thinking further about this, it occurred to me one evening when in conversation with two friends and fellow boat owners, that most weekends we skippers actually compete with each other for the same tiny handful of individuals from our membership pool for people we want to invite to crew on our boats. In other words, suitable crewing candidates constituted a tiny elite.

So what's the cause of this crazy situation?

The painful truth that became apparent as soon as I started probing was that the vast majority of the available members simply have not got the qualities that most skippers are looking for in their crew, though this, I believe, is mainly due to ignorance on the part of these recruits. If that is your problem, in many cases you can rectify this by absorbing the information in this book. However, I have a suspicion the issue originally stems from a lack of conscious awareness on the part of the would-be crewing candidates.

The ideas in this book aim to fill in some of the missing information, and to help well-meaning crewing candidates develop some of that missing awareness. Skippers will benefit as well, simply by understanding what's missing and maybe by giving a copy of this book to newcomers before they come aboard their vessels.

Here's the rub: Most novices to yachting simply do not realise what is required of them.

My aim is to try to give newcomers some basic ideas and principles so they can develop the necessary qualities in themselves. There is a kind of ironic joke question in yachting circles that goes like this:

Question: "How long does it take for the average person to learn to sail?"
Answer: "The average person never learns to sail."

Sailing demands special personal qualities, like any adventure sport (for example mountaineering), and this will almost certainly require every novice sailor to dig deep inside to find some extra inner resources he or she may never have realised they have because they are lying dormant. A very few seem to sense this instinctively, but the majority are sadly unaware of it. You have to be self-sufficient and self-motivated in your mindset, yet at the same time willing to be a team player, as well as eager to learn. In short you must become your best self, and if you are not prepared to develop those qualities and participate wholeheartedly, better to be honest with yourself and stay at home.

Skippering a boat requires considerable multi-tasking so the average skipper, while perfectly happy to teach willing subjects, has neither the time nor the inclination to be your nanny. Many novice crew fear that they will let themselves down because of their lack of knowledge of sailing. If so, they are looking in the wrong place because no skipper in his or her right mind expects a novice to have sailing skills or knowledge – that's understood. But if you are willing to learn and pay attention and contribute without having to be cajoled, the skipper will love you to pieces and you will enjoy yourself.

- ♠ Most novice would-be crew have no idea what is expected of them and therefore don't even realise they don't fit with most skipper's requirements.

- ♠ Many people who have never been on a boat before display a curious unconsciousness or unawareness in the way they behave when aboard that leaves most skippers gasping in disbelief and frustration.

This is not rocket science, as I say skippers don't expect newcomers to the sport to know anything about sailing. That's not the point. I'm talking about common sense and domestic issues that apply just as much at home as afloat and do not require any nautical knowledge whatsoever, a sort of awareness of, and sensitivity to, the needs of others and of yourself as well, a kind of pro-active willingness to use your brain to think ahead and to think of others *without having to be told.*

While a community of more than one aboard a boat is certainly not a democracy – in fact it's an autocracy – cruising under sail is most definitely a team effort and any crew's efficient functioning is in no small part down to the leadership ability of the skipper. But each crew member has to play a fulsome and enthusiastic part too if everyone is to enjoy the experience. And enjoyment, naturally, is what it's all about.

In short it's all about *attitude, attitude, attitude.*

As I said, most new members who are novices to yachting simply do not understand what is required of them, and you could argue that we skippers are arrogant in expecting them to. Whether that be true or not, this book tries to remedy the matter by giving you, as a newcomer to sailing, some basic ideas and principles so you can develop the necessary qualities in yourself. If you put them into practise you'll have no shortage of opportunities to get afloat.

This might sound cruel, but let me explain from the skipper's point of view. I used to belong to a club that rarely holds races. It comprises mainly members who want to cruise local waters at weekends, though once or twice a year some of us ventured further afield on an extended cruise. Our weekends are precious and we do not want to waste them doing favours for people we do not get along with. Moreover, the club is not a sailing school and many of our skippers have not the foggiest idea how to teach new aspirants in clear, simple and concise ways. Of course they will have to explain what they want done, though sometimes that task can be delegated to another more experienced crew member. The important point I am trying to get across is that most skippers strongly feel they should never have to coach anybody in basic social skills.

Now that I am retired and keep my boat in France, I'm on board for much longer periods – perhaps six weeks in the summer. That has made me even more picky about who I sail with because I might be confined with someone not just for a weekend but for a week or more. If there's a personality clash it's a nightmare.

I repeat, a lack of sailing skills is rarely the problem, though that may sound odd, for the fundamentals of conducting a vessel under sail can be imparted one way or another quite quickly to a willing recipient. It's the human relations' side of the activity where things can easily fall apart.

It's very easy to put people off sailing if they start with negative experiences, as I repeatedly tell some of my more intolerant skipper friends, and that's a shame. Nevertheless, most skippers are willing to train novice crew patiently *as long as they show willing*. Do not expect to be mollycoddled.

Imagine you are invited to a party near your home. You turn up at the appointed time bringing with you a bottle of wine, and perhaps a salad for the buffet. That, you believe, is your contribution to the party, so you go and sit quietly in the corner for a while.

Now if all the guests did the same, what an excruciatingly dull party it would be. No one is giving anything of themselves.

The essence of a good party, apart from the music, the food and perhaps the alcohol, is social intercourse. Genuine connections or interactions between people are what it's all about. Cruising under sail is exactly the same in principle – you have to give something of yourself, from your heart, full bloodedly, on a continuous basis. Selfishness, or what psychologists call narcissism, is definitely out within the confines of a boat. There has to be a rapport with everyone on board.

What the skipper gives you as crew is an opportunity to know the joy of the sailing experience. It costs us a small fortune to keep our boats moored and maintained, but what most of us want in return is not money. Most of the skippers I know want active, willing participation at all levels, not passengers. And I am not necessarily talking about physical ability or prowess – most people with disabilities are just as capable of contributing something valuable as the able bodied, and almost invariably do.

This is the bottom line as the vast majority of skippers see it, myself included: if you are not prepared to participate and contribute qualities you have deep inside, your efforts will be a waste of everyone's time, for you will not be invited more than once to come on board as crew. But I must reiterate, *do not be put off by a lack of sailing skills or knowledge.* Instead, be prepared to learn.

The following true story beautifully illustrates my point about using common sense and communicating honestly. Only the name has been changed:

DAVE ROBSON

Some years ago one fine spring morning I set sail with a young lad who had been helping me with some maintenance, from Bembridge in the Isle of Wight to visit Cherbourg on the North coast of France on the other side of the English Channel, a passage of some twelve hours when the conditions are good and the wind is in the right direction, which they both were.

After a very enjoyable sail that lasted all day we entered Cherbourg Marina at about 8.00 p.m. French time, just as it was starting to get dark, and went ashore for a delightful meal. Later we returned to the boat and went to bed, Mike on one of the saloon berths and I in the forward cabin.

Next morning I awoke at about 6.00 a.m. to find my crew sitting doubled over in the saloon where he had been trying to sleep without much success, wearing a heavy pullover, hugging himself and shivering severely.

"Where's your sleeping bag Michael?" I asked him.

"I didn't bring one," he replied.

I was flabbergasted! How could anyone be so stupid?

"But we went through this twice on the phone last week, what you should bring, and I specifically mentioned to bring a sleeping bag twice," I uttered in exasperation. "Why didn't you bring it? And why didn't you tell me you hadn't brought it? I warned you it would be cold at night."

"I thought I could buy one on the way," Mike replied sheepishly.

My mouth fell open. I was aghast. We had sailed some seventy-five miles from England to France and much of that time we'd been out of sight of land, entirely surrounded by water. Where on earth did he expect to find a shop in the middle of the English Channel that would sell him a sleeping bag? It might sound like a funny story, but sleep deprivation coupled with a danger of hypothermia is not a pretty combination on a boat. Moreover, a very tired crew is more of a liability than a help. True the sun was now rising in the sky and soon we'd feel like toast, which would solve the immediate problem, but I felt I had been dumped with a situation that would become a crisis again as soon as darkness fell *because my crew had failed to take responsibility for his own well-being,* and I was angry at his thoughtlessness and crass stupidity.

I tried to make allowances to myself for the fact that he was a young boy of 17 and very shy and inexperienced in the ways of the world, but a nagging feeling persisted that I had still not been told the whole truth, so I probed further. In the end Mike finally admitted the real reason he hadn't brought a sleeping bag was because he didn't own one and he couldn't afford to buy one, but was too embarrassed to admit it. This at least made more sense.

"But Mike, if you'd told me that, I could have borrowed one for you from a friend, or you could have used the spare one I keep under my bunk in the forward cabin."

I went and got it out forthwith. The immediate problem of the sleeping bag was solved, but the ongoing situation of a potentially worrisome crew remained. What problematic situation would Mike create next, I wondered? You may think I'm exaggerating, but if someone displays childish or irresponsible behaviour on a boat they immediately define themselves as a potential danger in the eyes of most skippers.

Of course I understood Mike's embarrassment in this situation, but failing to flag up a difficulty does not make a problem go away. It was a very real problem and it had to be solved because later that day we were due to sail somewhere else away from home and if it were not, a similar situation would obviously arise again at nightfall. Luckily I had a spare sleeping bag aboard so in this case the solution was easy.

Unable to sleep properly because he was too cold, Mike had suffered a miserable night for no good reason and I had been presented with an unnecessary problem because he had failed to communicate something important about himself and his equipment regarding this cruise that had clearly been troubling him.

It may sound cruel, but when you agree to go sailing on someone's boat, there is a tacit, unwritten agreement that you will take care of yourself properly so that as far as possible you remain "fit for purpose," as it were. If you don't know how to do that – ask your skipper *before* a problem develops. He may be depending on you.

It takes a certain maturity to tell the truth when you feel embarrassed, but never forget embarrassing situations can quickly become life-threatening issues on a boat, or at the very least irritating in the extreme. You must square up to them and deal with them full on as they arise.

Because I'd already told Mike twice in advance to bring a sleeping bag I refused to feel guilty for his misfortune, but there's no getting away from the fact that a skipper's primary duty is to take overall responsibility for whatever happens on his boat, so I felt bad that he'd had an unpleasant, freezing cold and sleepless night even though I knew it wasn't my fault.

That's the whole point. Even if he doesn't feel *guilty,* a skipper feels *responsible* and that's why he doesn't take kindly to incidents like this which potentially sabotage his best endeavours to keep everyone safe and happy through thoughtlessness or irresponsible behaviour. Moreover, like it or not, most of the skippers I know are perfection fanatics and control freaks – they take pride in making everything go perfectly and don't like having their egos bruised by having something go wrong, even if it's someone else's fault.

This in brief is how the vast majority of skippers see it:

♠ If you are not prepared to contribute human social qualities in an open, genuine way, you're better off staying at home.

♠ If you are unwilling or unable to take responsibility for your own sensible and safety-conscious behaviour, better to stay ashore in the pub.

In either case you will not be invited more than once to come on board as crew.

In the following chapters we look in more detail at what this means in practice.

CHAPTER TWO

ATTITUDE, ATTITUDE, ATTITUDE

You've either got them or you haven't.
I refer to the two essential basic qualities that cannot be taught, but which you can develop in yourself once you perceive the need, and if you have the motivation. They are the two magic ingredients that make everyone want to sail with you.

No, I am not talking about ability, knowledge, experience, agility, strength, cooking skills, joke-making capacity, wealth, good eyesight or even sex appeal. I'm talking about *attitude* and *awareness,* plain and simple.

If you have a positive *attitude* and you make yourself *aware* of what is going on, not just on a technical boating level, but in terms of how you conduct yourself and your human relationships with the people around you, then the other qualities listed above, such as sailing ability, can be viewed as very useful and much appreciated added extras, like the icing on a cake. But if your attitude is negative and you do not cultivate self-awareness and boat-awareness, there *is* no cake.

This is the importance of what I'm saying: You can be the most skilful sailor in the world, but if you have a negative attitude and a lack of self-awareness and boat-awareness, very few people will want to sail with you. But with a positive attitude and a reasonable level of awareness, people will invite you aboard whether you know how to sail or not. With a positive attitude you will soon learn to make a useful contribution and your awareness will grow, and the more that happens the more you will learn and enjoy your sailing and the more people will want to sail with you. It's pure cause and effect and it really is that simple.

I have had the misfortune to sail on unharmonious boats and I can assure you, it's not in the least bit enjoyable, no matter how great the boat, how terrific the sailing conditions or how beautiful the environment. I certainly wouldn't want to repeat the experience.

Here's a classic example of what can happen: if you go below to make yourself a cup of tea and don't bother to ask if anyone else wants one, that simply shows you do not care about your fellow shipmates, and there is nothing worse for destroying harmonious sailing relationships than being perceived as narcissistic and not caring about the others. This is the important point – sailing ability is not the issue for, as I said, nobody expects a novice to know how to sail. But by definition you are experienced in being a human being, therefore for this kind of unconscious behaviour there is no excuse, not even from a novice sailor.*

Many novice crew members seem to think that yachting is an esoteric art cloaked in mystique and only for the initiated, and in many respects that is exactly what it is. But for the intelligent aspirant there is always an open door, for the simple reason that many aspects of boating are common sense, meaning that no boating knowledge is required before a newcomer can quickly become a valued contributor. As a novice there is no need to feel intimidated, for there are many ways to make yourself useful.

A genuine desire to contribute.
Part of the positive attitude of which I speak is an important quality to bring to any yachting trip, and that's a

---

* All the examples quoted in this book are true incidents that have happened to me, either when skippering, when crewing for other skippers, or as a student on sailing school boats with other students and a skipper/instructor, in some cases more often than I care to remember.

genuine desire to contribute something useful. If you do that consistently, you will be making the skipper's life much easier and more enjoyable and you'll start scoring brownie points like mad! I am talking about a willingness here, not a sycophantic effort to ingratiate yourself as skipper's pet – that simply puts everyone's back up, introduces tension and gets people reaching for the vomit bags. Just remain relaxed but alert, ready to learn, and be pro-active – that will do fine.

At this point it's worth asking yourself if you feel you really, honestly, *do* have a genuine desire to contribute, even though you might feel nervous and inhibited because of your lack of knowledge and experience. If you don't, then the whole thing becomes a pointless exercise and you might as well go away and pursue another sport that you do feel passionate about.

If on the other hand you wish to overcome your misgivings and jump in, then it becomes a case of *"Feel the Fear and Do It Anyway,"* as the author Susan Jeffers put it.

Human psychology is a vital factor in determining whether a sailing trip is enjoyable or not. Cruising under sail is an affair of the heart and a community activity, so if your contribution does not come from your heart, it is worthless – *and skippers can tell the difference, even if sometimes they don't realise it.* It is worth remembering that sailing is entirely unnecessary and pointless, we do it purely for the joy of doing it, and that is precisely why it is so addictive to certain kinds of people like me and other skippers who I know.

The only possible purposes for going sailing are the enjoyment and the spiritual nourishment that derives from communing with nature and your fellow beings and, of course, the mental and physical challenges. With this in mind, try to imagine the following three scenarios:

Scenario 1: You do the washing-up without being asked, with a willingness and a smile on your face, because you sincerely want to help keep the boat shipshape. You might hate washing up at home, but your regard for your fellows and their needs, coupled with your respect for the boat and for yourself mean you do it with pleasure, even though it might not be your turn. The others instinctively pick this up and you will immediately start to be respected as a responsible and promising addition to the ship's company.

Scenario 2: It's no use pretending to be happy if you hate what you are doing, for human psychology being what it is, most astute skippers can sniff out a reluctant or resentful washer-upper at a thousand paces. If you broadcast an atmosphere of resentment while doing said washing-up, even if you have not been asked to do it, there will be few credits, even though the skipper is relieved the washing up got done and he didn't have to do it himself. The problem is you put out a feeling of repressed anger that you might not even be aware of, and that's unpleasant for everyone, even though they might not be aware of what they are receiving. It makes people feel uneasy. Feelings, be they positive or negative, spoken or unspoken, conscious or unconscious, are magnified substantially within the confines of a yacht.

Scenario 3: The third possibility is that you always disappear at washing-up time, or remain seated and let someone else do it. This is instantly perceived as shirking your responsibilities and once again not caring for your fellows or the general welfare of the boat. Result – not only no brownie points, but very likely minus brownie points.

These simple examples illustrate how, though the basics of domesticity may seem trivial and not worth mentioning, trust me, these sorts of incidents can become huge issues. Bad vibes or drooping morale on a boat are a skipper's worst enemy, and they have a habit of spreading unless sorted out fast. When it happens it quite simply mars everyone's boating experience. Always remember – even the most hardened racing crews do this for enjoyment, perhaps with the exception of the elite professionals. Most skippers will agree, as soon as it ceases to be enjoyable, it's time to call it a day and try again next time – *with a different crew!*

If you find yourself re-enacting Scenario 2, try asking yourself what's bothering you, or could you change your attitude? *Once you become aware of what you are doing you can consciously choose to change your attitude, and thereby your behaviour.* In fact you can even change your beliefs or mindset so you begin to appreciate your washing-up task as valuable and supportive to your team and skipper rather than menial and beneath your dignity. That's what my friends who practise NLP (Neuro-Linguistic Programming) call reframing. You look at the same thing in a different, more positive way to accentuate the benefits in your own mind. This is the real secret – w*hen you change your mindset, your behaviour and your body language change automatically.*

I hope, if you are sufficiently interested in crewing to be reading this book, that you will never allow yourself to slip into Scenario 3. If you realise you are doing that, it's time to acknowledge you've got a serious attitude problem and to wake up and smell the coffee. Even better, get up and *make* the coffee *for everyone.*

Now here's something else to be super-aware about: There's another mistake that even happy washer-uppers sometimes fall foul of, and that's being too "nice" and *always* doing the washing-up, allowing other crew members to skive off and avoid the job. This is the opposite extreme when what we want is a reasonable balance.

Overdoing it is not at all a good idea because allowing yourself to be exploited does not earn you respect and it also gives the impression you do not have the confidence to do (or learn) any other jobs on the boat, or you just want to please everybody because you feel insecure.

This may or may not be true of you, but if you are lacking in confidence and/or knowledge, it becomes more important than ever, after you have done your share of the domestics down below, to get your backside out on deck and into the fresh air to *demonstrate a willingness to learn new skills.* You cannot build up confidence in all-round crewing tasks unless you come up on deck and get stuck in.

The average cruising yacht skipper wants multi-skilled and multi-tasking crew members, not just folk who never progress beyond the domestics (this is not to denigrate the importance of those latter tasks). It is also important for your own enjoyment and self-esteem to avoid getting typecast as a galley slave. Apart from that, there will also be times when you need to take your turn to get some rest, recuperation and relaxation while someone else washes up.

Domestic tasks assume disproportionate importance when co-existing on a boat because they can become highly emotive issues, as can every other aspect of living aboard, when someone has a negative attitude. One person dragging his or her feet can quickly escalate into a flashpoint for ugly confrontations. Your *attitude* towards helping keep the boat ship-shape plays a significant part in building up an overall good impression of you in the eyes of the skipper and everyone else on board.

A positive attitude helps to develop harmony and teamwork on board and influences others to be positive too. If you have to be asked to do something every time it's your turn, and then you do it grudgingly, this inevitably contributes towards creating an "atmosphere". In truth, the willingness is more important than getting the actual task done (though of course, tasks do have to get done, and sometimes urgently).

Vital though they are, harmony, willingness, motivation and positive attitude are not taught in conventional sailing schools – and they should not have to be. If you are the resistant type yet you want to be invited again and again, it's down to you to work on your attitude.

Here's another classic scenario:

The ship's company wakes up in the morning in harbour and you are sleeping in the saloon. On the vast majority of cruising yachts the saloon is a bedroom at night and a living/dining room and kitchen during the day and a navigation station at all times. It also acts as an access route from one end of the boat's interior to the other. You need to be mindful of this if your berth is in the saloon.

You get out of bed and go ashore for a shower, but you leave your unrolled sleeping bag lying around on your bunk, together with your dirty underpants, sopping wet smelly socks from yesterday's heavy weather passage and your bag half off the bunk with stuff spilling out of it all over the floor. Sound familiar?

This will become an instant source of annoyance, for once people start to rouse themselves the saloon is no longer a dormitory, it is now the communal living room and dining room, and in most cases an extension to the kitchen, and you have in effect disappeared leaving a mess for the others to live with.

It's probably most irritating for the person who tries to sit down and gets a wet bum from sitting on your soggy socks, and for the next person after that who sits down after the socks have been removed but who also gets a wet bum because the bunk is now wet. *Even if your bunk is in a separate cabin, it is your responsibility to keep it civilised, and your gear under control.*

But perhaps the most maddening thing of all that can happen when your allocated sleeping space is the saloon, and this doesn't apply so much on long passages where you continue sailing through the night, is you failing to get up reasonably quickly in the morning when the ship's company starts to stir. The reason why this is a problem is because once sleeping is over, you and your gear constitute an obstruction if you don't get out of bed and tidy up your stuff.

Moreover, if the reason you can't or won't get up is because you went a pint too far in the pub the night before, don't expect any sympathy from the others. On the contrary, expect even more irritation, especially if you are the only one with a hangover, for your behaviour will be considered irresponsible and your suffering your own fault!

Most experienced sailors don't suffer fools gladly and they especially don't like it when your problem becomes their problem too.

If you are not a morning person and you tend to wake up grumpy, please don't come sailing on my boat. If there's good reason for you to be grumpy later – say something untoward happens like we run aground – I can cope with that, but first thing in the morning is a highly sensitive time for most people and the last thing I and most of my fellow sailors want at such a time is somebody's bad moods.

If that's you, go ashore, have a shower and come back when you're ready to think about the ship and her company, and not just about yourself. But for heaven's sake tidy up and stow your gear first!

I daresay you can tell by now that I won't put up with childish behaviour on my boat, but believe it or not I'm one of the most tolerant skippers I know! It's that over the years, from bitter experience, I have become very choosy about who sails with me on my boat, and that's why I honestly do know of what I speak. Like most skippers, I'm delighted to embrace intelligent, considerate and enthusiastic fellow sailors happily and with appropriate hospitality.

Now some of the skippers I've sailed with over the years have themselves been very messy and bad tempered, even curmudgeonly in one case. If you end up on their boat it's for you to decide whether or not to sail with that person again.

I once sailed in someone's boat, somewhere on the East Coast of England, which was so filthy and badly maintained that even his tools and all the stainless steel fittings were rusty! Below decks was like the black hole of Calcutta and I refused to go down there except when I had to go to the toilet. Thank heavens it was only a day out. I heard later that his boat had subsequently sunk on its river moorings because the skipper had gone home neglecting to close the toilet seacock, which was so leaky it let in water. Never again did I sail with that gentleman. Neither would I have him on my boat.

Even on a properly maintained and reasonably clean boat of course it's entirely possible that your skipper might wake up in a bad mood. As long as it doesn't happen too often he can probably get away with it because that's the nature of an autocracy I'm afraid. It's his prerogative! Just humour him a bit and he'll get over it (probably), or better still, leave him alone for a while.

Never forget, most good skippers are utter control freaks – they believe they have earned that right – and many are fastidious about everything on board being just right.

Consideration for fellow crew members when confined in a tiny space is paramount. You must look after yourself and take full personal responsibility, but also you must take into account the needs of *all* the others – even the super-cool guy you can't stand because all the girls in the harbours you visit fancy him and not you.

There is nothing more depressing than wet and dampness below decks, especially in cold, miserable weather. So when you go off watch and go below from the cockpit in your sopping waterproofs, *don't sit down, and don't wander back and forth through the boat.* Take your wet stuff off first and leave it in the "wet area" (ask the skipper where that is). That shows consideration, and helps you feel more comfortable too. If you really don't want to take your wet gear off because you are shortly going back on deck, stay in the wet area yourself.

These things may seem subtle, but I assure you – skippers register them, even if they don't realise, and it makes all the difference when it comes to crew selection time. Skippers always prefer people who will help make a cruise go smoothly, and they avoid like the plague the chap (or woman) who gave them trouble last time. A good reputation gets your crewing diary crammed with commitments – a bad one leaves you propping up the yacht club bar on your own!

At this point it might be a really good idea to sit down quietly and ask yourself some deeply searching questions, such as *"How do I feel about all this?"*, *"What sort of a person* am I?", "Am I honestly suited to this?", "Are there things about myself I need to change or work on?"

Please note the first question asks, "How do I feel …?" not "What do I think …?" That's the Life Coach in me coming out. The reason why that's a vitally important distinction is because *the voice of your heart always knows your truth,* and that's what matters in a case like this. When you ask yourself, *"how do I feel …?"* the answer comes from your heart if you are being brutally honest with yourself. But if you ask yourself, *"what do I think?",* the answer comes from your mind. You need to know how you *feel* because there's no point trying to fool yourself, if you can't enjoy the sailing experience for what it is, warts and all, there's no point to it.

If, after this exercise in self-enquiry, you find you are enjoying yourself and you feel yourself being pulled to do more of it, now you know what qualities to cultivate more strongly to get invited back.

Now for another sensitive subject. I once chartered a boat with some friends in the Grenadine Islands of the Caribbean and because of the hot climate very soon it became apparent that one of the crew had a personal hygiene problem, though to be honest, it was us who had the problem, not him, because no one had the courage to tell him about it.

He was also a messy creature and before long his cabin was like a bear pit – so much so that the guy who was sharing it with him took to sleeping outside in the cockpit tucked under the spray hood to get away from the suffocating squalor of the cabin.

I found out about this after a few days when a strange odour reached my cabin, which was at the other end of the 50 foot boat! It did not take too long to guess where the smell was coming from and when I opened his cabin door I was almost overcome by the fumes, which were not unlike how I would expect a Brazilian favela to smell, or perhaps the stagnant backwaters of Venice in the height of summer.

He was such a nice chap and he was having such a good time, everyone was too embarrassed to tackle him on the subject, so what did we do? We waited till he went ashore, opened every hatch and door on the boat and sprayed his cabin thoroughly with air freshener. Sadly, I also made a mental note never to invite him to come sailing with us again because I didn't want the unpleasant pong, and neither did I want the embarrassment.

Now of course I would not dream of suggesting that any readers of this book would fall into such a category, but nevertheless please take my point in the spirit in which it is intended, the sad truth is that many of our expectant and eager would-be crew, vital new blood for our beloved sport of sailing, will not ever reach square one in the invitation stakes, so for them the game can never begin in earnest. If you find yourself struggling to get to first base for whatever reason, here are some suggestions:

- ♠ When your skipper says it's time to get out of bed, get out of bed.

- ♠ Be genuinely willing to participate in all the crewing tasks on the boat, not just the cooking and washing-up, from the moment you get out of bed.

- ♠ Don't be the one who shies away from the domestic chores.

- ♠ Always clean up after yourself and keep your stuff tidy and properly stowed.

- ♠ Look after your personal hygiene but remember, on a boat, fresh water, battery power and gas are precious commodities which can soon be exhausted. Do not waste them and, if in doubt, always ask the skipper *beforehand* if it's OK to use some. This is especially important when anchored away from shore facilities, and again, it shows you care.

- ♠ Every night before turning in, ask the skipper what time he wants to leave harbour next morning, put your alarm on and be ready, showered, fully clothed and equipped, five minutes before the time he says. Do not wait till three minutes before departure to rush ashore to the toilets and showers.

♠ Take personal responsibility for conducting yourself like a mature human being and *always* consider your fellows on board, even your weary, battle scarred and much maligned skipper, who is, or should be, doing his best to look after *your* safety and wellbeing. Although it is the skipper's responsibility to ensure your welfare, he is no one's nanny and he certainly should not have to do your thinking for you. Nor is he your social worker, nor your psychotherapist, nor even – dare I say it – your Life Coach!

♠ **Awareness, awareness, awareness!** Especially on deck, always be aware of what is going on, that if you do not concentrate on what you are doing you might get hit by the boom, you might fall overboard, when steering you might wander off course and run aground or hit something, you might cause injury to yourself or others. Many people get spaced out and others behave erratically or get frozen with fear when underway. This is a nightmare for the skipper because these people are his responsibility and he has to constantly watch them like a hawk lest they endanger themselves or others.

♠ Be *aware* that your *unawareness* can endanger yourself and others.

♠ Continue your awareness when stepping ashore with lines (some finger pontoons can be very narrow, bouncy, wet, slippery from bird droppings, or even icy), when tackling quayside ladders, walking on pontoons or harbour walls or anywhere near the water. I once climbed off a boat after being on board for a month and almost stepped out straight in front of a passing car ...

♠ **Never argue with the skipper**, especially when you detect a sense of urgency in his orders, unless you are absolutely convinced he is about to put the vessel or its crew in danger. Arguing, especially with the skipper, causes immense irritation and can be seriously counter-productive, especially in a crisis.

♠ Always tell the skipper *beforehand* if you have a medical or health condition, however minor, bring any relevant medication with you, and don't forget to use it when necessary. Half way across the English Channel in a force nine with wind on the nose is not the time to tell him you had a triple bypass operation last week and were told to rest and recuperate. Nor will you find a chemist for your vitamin C tablets anywhere near the shipping separation zone.

♠ Always tell the skipper *beforehand* of any dietary requirements. It's no good announcing you are a kosher vegan halal vegetarian with food allergies and macrobiotic preferences when he plonks your steak and chips on the saloon table.

♠ Make sure you are suitably equipped for the climate where you are going. In the UK even in the height of summer you need to be prepared for all four seasons in one day.

♠ Your skipper should not have to tell you to put on a pullover when he sees you shivering. You must look after yourself properly or you soon become a liability. Put the pullover on *before* you get cold, and don your waterproof gear *before* your clothes get wet, otherwise it's too late.

♠ If you are going to a warm or hot place, such as the Mediterranean or the Caribbean, take plenty of sun block as well as high factor suntan cream, Calamine lotion, a couple of long-sleeved shirts, a hat with an all-round brim, sunglasses and the strongest insect repellent you can find, and use all of them.

♠ Never bring a suitcase onto a boat – always use a soft squashy bag – and never wear high-healed or leather-soled shoes, or any kind of shoes that slip on wet surfaces. This can be highly dangerous.

♠ Never bring illegal drugs, firearms, fireworks or explosives on board and always ask the skipper where, if anywhere, you can smoke and drink alcohol.

♠ When the skipper says wear a lifejacket and/or harness – **DO IT.** Never argue, delay or make excuses as to why you think you don't need to. Follow all safety instructions precisely. If you die or get injured, the skipper is responsible.

♠ I always tell my crew, be they novices or old timers, *"always think safety before you do anything"*. This alone will considerably reduce your risk of having an accident.

♠ Find something strong to hold onto when it's rough, and even in calm conditions, and always remember the axiom that has always held good for me, *"one hand for yourself, one hand for the boat."*

♠ Another piece of advice that has also proved itself time and time again over the years – always take at least one set of long-sleeved and long-legged thermal underwear with you when you go sailing, even in the height of summer. If you do that, you'll be prepared for anything.

I could go on for many more pages, but I hope I have said enough by now to demonstrate the importance of the matters we have covered so far. Like I said, it's all common sense.

OK, now we've got all that settled we can move onto other topics aimed at making you the most wanted crew in your yacht club ...

***

(According to research carried out a long time ago by the RYA, the single issue that concerns the majority of novices when stepping aboard a yacht for the first time is not "is the boat seaworthy?" or "is the skipper competent?", as one might expect, but "how does the toilet work?" I just thought I'd share that with you).

CHAPTER THREE

BE SURE TO CHOOSE A GOOD SKIPPER

Sadly, not all skippers are reliable, or trustworthy with your life, and their boats are not necessarily as seaworthy or well-maintained as we would like. Also there is a possibility you and the skipper simply don't like each other, in which case the two of you can never strike up a good rapport.

Choose your skipper carefully – ask the right questions and always trust your instincts. One you've left harbour it's too late for qualms, and your allegiance has to be unquestionable. Be warned, if you do not take the trouble to find out a little about the person to whom you are entrusting your life, you are hitch-hiking with a total stranger and your experience may not be as happy as you had hoped. Needless to say, I learned this the hard way.

Early in the days when I was trying to master the more basic practical skills inherent in the subtle art of yachting, I joined the Cruising Association. At the time, this estimable body owned the largest nautical library in the British Isles, and there was a chart room where members could go to plan passages in any part of the world. The collection of pilotage books and charts literally covered the entire globe.

Not only was the place a mine of information, there was also a crew register, a sort of matchmaking service for skippers and crews, a good programme of social and educational events, an excellent bar and, most important, the organisation's headquarters was in London and therefore accessible to me. What I was after was more opportunities for crewing experience, increased knowledge and understanding about yachting, and more contacts in the world of cruising under sail, especially among skippers who might need crew.

One evening, at a Skippers and Crew meeting, I met a skipper who wanted crew to join him to participate in a race starting in Cowes in the Isle of Wight at the end of Cowes Week that year and ending at Dartmouth on the south coast of Devon, and in my naïve innocence I signed up to join the crew. The trip was a nightmare from beginning to end.

We were told to meet at Shamrock Quay, a marina in the Itchen River at Southampton, at a certain time in the afternoon of the day before the race so we could motor the boat down Southampton Water and across the Solent to Cowes to watch the firework display that traditionally celebrates the end of Cowes week. "Sounds like a plan," I thought to myself.

I joined the assembled company at the appointed hour at the Waterfront bar in the aforementioned marina and we waited for the skipper to arrive. And we waited, and we waited, and we waited until, some three hours late, and with hardly an apology, he turned up saying he'd been getting provisions (which turned out to be mostly an awful lot of tins of beer) at the nearby supermarket.

This we promptly loaded aboard his boat with our gear and made ready to leave the marina, which we did as soon as we could.

Of course, although we went hell for leather down Southampton Water, we missed the firework display and found a berth for the night somewhere in Cowes.

Next morning found us out in Cowes Roads looking for the start line and hoisting sails. Our helmsman chosen by the skipper for the start was the only person on board who was a qualified RYA Yachtmaster, allegedly very experienced in the art of yacht racing, and the first thing he did, when jockeying for position on the start line, was to hit a huge red metal navigational buoy, conspicuously positioned in plain sight in the middle of Cowes Roads, a glancing blow with the port (left) side of our hull. Unperturbed, we sailed on.

I was already beginning to get a sinking feeling (no pun intended) in the pit of my stomach. The collision had been entirely due to the helmsman's negligence and failure to think ahead. We'd all assumed he knew what he was doing, but we were already beginning to have doubts, and the race hadn't even started.

Eventually we heard the gun and we were off, flying westwards along the Solent on an exhilarating, lively beat to windward with a fair tide under us towards the Needles. It was only shortly before we reached Hurst Castle (we'd covered a distance of some ten miles) that the skipper realised we'd made an error at the start by failing to round another red buoy near the start on the correct side, and unless we went back and rounded it correctly, we would be disqualified. We were not yet past the Isle of Wight! This we all knew would cost us at least five hours.

Disaster followed disaster. We sailed back slowly to Cowes against the tide, rounded the buoy correctly and set off again towards the Needles. By this time the tide had turned and we founding ourselves slogging to windward against it again, this time in a westerly direction, and making slow progress. Of course we'd lost sight of all the other competitors a long time before that and unsurprisingly we never saw them again.

Somehow we got through the Needles channel and sailed across Poole Bay, properly on our way west at last. Something I really didn't like was that this boat had many ropes lead back to the cockpit but instead of coiling up the long tails of rope neatly to keep the cockpit tidy and the ropes untangled, the person pulling in the line would simply throw the tail down the companionway onto the cabin floor so when you went below it was like walking on a bed of snakes and very easy to turn your ankle.

Added to this, the skipper and crew consumed a considerable quantity of beer while on passage and their habit was to drop the empty can on the cockpit floor and just leave it there for anyone to stumble on. This kind of sloppy behaviour not only leads to a squalid feeling on the boat, but it invites accidents. It also feels non-caring in the extreme.

The skipper, who was a very gung-ho young chap, boasted continuously about how well he knew his wonderful carbon-fibre vessel and how easily he could move around it almost blindfold, even underway, but as we were crossing Lyme Bay the sea began to cut up rough and he called for everyone to don his or her lifejacket and to attach their safety harness lines to the boat. He, being the giant ego that he was, refused to wear his own lifejacket and attach his harness line on the grounds that he knew exactly what he was doing and he knew the boat.

Well of course you've guessed it. The only person who went overboard was him, or at least he would have done had I not caught hold of his ankle as he went over the side. And there he hung, dangling upside down over the side of his boat, bereft of any of the dignity he believed he had mustered by being a macho-man, until two more crew members arrived to help me pull him back on board.

I suggested politely but in the strongest possible terms that he now put on his lifejacket and affix his harness line but he still refused and, blow me down, exactly the same thing happened again about ten minutes later! Another rogue wave hit the side of the hull, there was a lurch and over he went. This time I'd been expecting it, though nobody else seemed at all worried, so fortunately I was standing in exactly the right spot to catch hold of his ankle again.

By the time we got the pig-headed idiot back on board I was thoroughly fed up, to put it bluntly, so I went below to have a bit of quiet time to myself sitting on the toilet, the one place I knew I'd be left alone. It was then, sitting is peaceful contemplation, that I heard a strange swishing sound under my feet and the awful realisation began to creep over me that we were taking in water somewhere, somehow.

Calmly finishing my business, I arose and lifted the floor of the toilet to find the entire bilge (under floor area of the hull) completely awash. This was very bad news which, needless to say I immediately reported to the skipper.

Of course the pathetically under capacity bilge pump could not cope, so there followed an hour of frantic bailing, followed by a session of trying to diagnose the problem. One thing I noticed was that we were taking in water only when we were on the starboard tack (heeled to port) but not when the boat was upright or heeled to starboard, so it was obvious that the leak was not below the waterline, thank heavens.

By this time I was beginning to suspect it had something to do with hitting the red buoy just outside of Cowes. But none of us could actually see anything amiss.

I suggested to the skipper, since we were obviously the last boat in the fleet by a long margin anyway, that we drop the sails to eliminate the heeling, motor in to the nearest harbour with repair facilities and call it a day, as any normal, sane person would do with a potentially sinking boat. "No no, we can't do that," he replied. "We'll be disqualified from the race if we put the engine on."

"What difference does it make," I spluttered in exasperation? "We're last. Everybody else has gone home already! What's the point of soldiering on in a leaking boat?"

"It's a matter of honour to finish the race correctly," he insisted. He was adamant we must sail on all the way to Dartmouth, trying to sail as much as possible on the port tack, and standing by to bail out if we had to turn to the starboard tack.

Finally, after what seemed an eternity, the fair town of Dartmouth hove into view and we identified the entrance to the beautiful River Dart. Then the wind dropped and I realised the nightmare wasn't over yet.

We just sat lolling about in the sunshine about a mile off the entrance, drifting helplessly backwards on the tide towards a group of anchored oil tankers. Yet still the skipper refused to start the engine.

Eventually after about ten minutes, when it became glaringly obvious we were going to hit one of the tankers if we allowed this to carry on, he abandoned his alleged honour, relented, motored into the river and found a pontoon berth, where we moored up and I was able to jump off this infernal boat from hell. From the pontoon we could clearly see a hairline crack about five feet in length along the port side of the hull a few inches above the waterline, exactly in the position where we'd hit the red buoy.

I'm afraid I wasn't going to hang around to help. I'd had more than enough of this loony skipper and his cavalier crew and five minutes after stepping ashore I was in a taxi to the railway station and then on a train to Southampton to pick up my car. I have never been so happy to step off a boat.

That was my first lesson in being careful to choose a great skipper, and not to assume that all skippers are competent. Your life can depend on getting this right.

A year or two later I went to another Skippers and Crew meeting at the Cruising Association, and that's where I met Charles (not his real name).

He had a very different proposition, he owned a lovely Sweden Yachts 41, a beautiful, powerful and spacious cruising yacht called *Caesar* (not her real name) in immaculate condition, which he'd been keeping on the Mediterranean coast of Spain. He wanted help to bring the boat back to Portsmouth. This looked like a wonderful mile-building opportunity and a chance to cruise the Atlantic coast of Europe. And, most important, it was not a race. I'd finally realised that yacht racing is far too stressful for my liking.

Charles was at least mindful of the weather forecast and flatly refused to leave any harbour in force six or stronger winds, which I thought very sensible, though because of that the whole trip took a month. He also preferred day sailing whenever possible, always finding a harbour in the evening, which also suited me because I wanted to explore ashore a little bit and sample the local gastronomy whenever possible.

Charles was a retired solicitor living on a handsome pension that he considered meagre. He was totally narcissistic and had to get his own way no matter what. Worst of all he showed scant if any regard for his crew. He insisted on going everywhere at seven knots, which meant often hoisting the mainsail and motor sailing at high revs into what were usually headwinds, often against the waves and tide, so although progress was fast, it felt like a slog much of the time.

He also had a habit of heading ashore to the most expensive restaurant in town, regardless of our pleas that we simply could not afford to do that every night. Not once in that whole month did Charles do any cooking on board. Indeed, he never made so much as a cup of tea, expecting his crew to behave like slaves in pandering to his every whim. He was in every way quite simply a martinet.

Because he was grossly obese, Charles did not like the boat heeling, which was another reason he preferred to motor sail when there was a headwind, and I wondered why he didn't trade in his sailing yacht for a powerboat. When he had to go below to the toilet when sailing or motor sailing to windward, we would have to luff up (turn the boat towards the wind) so she would lose power, slow down and come upright, very frustrating when you're zooming along in a merry breeze and a nice groove.

On many occasions we were stuck in harbour for several days waiting for strong weather to subside and, because of his wartime military experience, Charles felt it was his bounden duty as skipper to "keep up morale." This he did by giving us meaningless jobs to do, for example polishing the already gleaming interior joinery, or getting into the dinghy to scrub around the waterline of the hull.

We the crew would have been perfectly happy for the opportunity to sit down occasionally, soak up some rays, relax and read a book for a while, for it was we who were doing all the exertion of crewing the boat while Charles barked commands from the wheel like a tinpot dictator.

There was nothing wrong with morale, but he was so impatient and unable to sit still for a moment, he tried to project onto us his need to keep busy. It was his lack of people skills that eventually led to drooping morale and feelings of resentment on the rare occasions that it occurred.

Perhaps the main problem was that he regarded it as a delivery trip and we crew regarded it as a holiday. So another lesson learned – before the start ask, what is the basis of the proposed sailing trip? Make sure your expectations and those of the skipper are as much as possible in alignment before choosing to sail together.

CHAPTER FOUR

WHAT'S THE DEAL?

When a skipper invites you to go sailing with him on his own boat, what financial expectations will fall on you?

Many skippers expect to share the day to day expenses equally with everyone on board, but this can vary, so a clear arrangement that everyone is happy with needs to be discussed and agreed in advance. It has to be appreciated that a boat owner has to cope with considerable expense to keep his boat properly maintained and moored. He or she is not a charity and their purpose is not to provide you with free holidays.

So what are day to day expenses?

Usually a skipper pays all his boatyard costs, such as maintenance and repairs, launching the boat, lifting it out, and the cost of his permanent mooring. Other expenses incurred during a sailing trip, such as provisioning, harbour dues in places visited, meals ashore and so forth are usually but not always considered as day-to-day expenses of which you are expected to pay your share. Whatever the arrangement, it should be agreed and understood in advance.

At this point, and I should emphasise that the following has happened to me on more than one occasion. There is nothing more irritating for a skipper than a crew member offering to buy the skipper a drink at the yacht club bar, only to find when it's time to pay that he or she has conveniently "forgotten" to bring his or her wallet.

I understand that many people who want to sail are hard-up, but if that is so then either save up *beforehand,* or admit your plight *beforehand,* or stay at home. Many of us have to save up for holidays – there's no shame in that. The guiding principle, as always, in creating and conducting happy and fruitful relationships, is transparency and being clear with your boundaries, especially around money.

Trust me, it's very easy to fall out over money. It's a very emotive issue and a boat is like a crucible. Everything is magnified and heated up within the confines of a boat.

So how much money should you take? Best to contact the skipper beforehand and ask him to guesstimate the costs, but bear in mind this is only a guide and you should always add a healthy margin of safety, especially if you are going abroad. Local currency can be invaluable in some places, but pretty much everywhere in Europe nowadays allows you to pay for most things with a credit or debit card and at some fuel berths in France where I keep my boat you can only pay by card, so I try to keep a mixture of Euros and a debit card, with a credit card in reserve for dire emergencies.

Another point to bear in mind is that in some countries, Japan for example, it can be quite hard to find a cash machine (ATM) even in downtown Tokyo, especially ones that accept foreign bank cards, and even in Europe there are some tiny harbours without ATMs and it can be a very long walk or taxi ride to the nearest town.

Sometimes on a boat there is a kitty into which everybody pays an equal share and then day-to-day expenses are paid for out of the kitty. It may need replenishing part way through the trip, in which case it's equal shares again, and if there is anything left at the end, the remaining money is reimbursed equally.

On some boats it is agreed that the skipper contributes an equal share to the kitty, and on others only the crew contributes. But what is vital is that someone other than the skipper looks after the fund and takes responsibility for it. If someone on board has accounting skills then they are the obvious candidate, but the maths should be blissfully simple so anyone could do it really.

One other important point – if the boat uses a kitty system it only really works with cash in the local currency, so ask in advance to work out how much cash you will need.

Another system is for someone other than the skipper to keep a tally of what is spent and who spent it so you can all settle up at the end.

One or two skippers I have met simply charge crew members a fixed amount to cover day-to-day expenses, but here a skipper must be careful because it could be construed he is operating a commercial vessel by charging people to go sailing, and unless he has a commercial endorsement and his boat complies with the code regulations, he could be in trouble. He might also be liable for income tax on the money he receives. Hence, this method is very rare!

Yet other crews simply take it in turns to buy rounds at the bar, and also to buy meals, provisions, mooring fees and diesel, but that tends to happen only among more affluent crews who probably don't mind if the outcome is unequal.

It's also a good idea to have an agreement, or at least an understanding, about expensive meals out. If crew members are expected to pay for themselves it's embarrassing for everyone if someone wants to go to the most expensive restaurant (as in the trip I did with Charles in the previous chapter) and others can't afford such extravagance. Talk to your skipper in advance to evaluate if a particular sailing trip will suit your financial situation.

Now here's another complication to watch out for. Who pays for the wine? If, like me, you drink very little alcohol but your boating companions enjoy a bottle of wine or two and a few beers with their dinner, is it fair you should be expected to contribute? The answer is that when dinner is over most people nowadays just share the total bill equally, allowing a little extra for a tip, and that is what is usually expected. No one who has just spent a hard and exhilarating day beating to windward can be bothered to sit down and work out differing contributions to a bill in a restaurant, so if you can't simply accept that you're almost certainly going to have an embarrassing problem. It's just one of those things you will probably have to accept graciously, like it or not. I flag this up so you are prepared.

If you're a member of a yacht club or your skipper belongs to a particular boating association, you might be participating in a regatta, after which you might find yourself seated at dinner with a whole bunch of yacht crews from boats that each have their own financial arrangements. When that happens either the club or other organising body will have fixed a price for the evening for each participant, or each boat will sit at their own table and gets their own bill. This means if you are on a boat owned by somebody less affluent you are less likely to get stung for the champagne ordered by those more prosperous members on a big prestigious boat.

This can be a very embarrassing, even highly emotive, subject and in all honesty I find it quite hard to write about because there are so many variables and differences of opinion about which way is best.

This is in no way meant to be a judgment, but the reality is that some echelons of the boating fraternity are very well off, which is why yachting is perceived to be an elitist sport. But actually the vast majority of people I meet in harbours as I cruise around are very down to earth and very conscious of what they are spending. The upshot is, if you don't want to be embarrassed it's a good idea to find out in advance what you are getting yourself into and choose an appropriate financial peer group with whom to go sailing.

If you are very lucky you might find a wealthy skipper who wants you on board and says he will pay for everything, which could also be embarrassing for different reasons. If that happens to you, all I can say is you'd better be on your best behaviour!

One more important point related to money, especially when sailing abroad, it's always a good idea to have medical insurance, or at the very least in Europe an EU medical card if you're a UK or EU citizen (this may become obsolete for British people after the UK leaves the European Union).

I would never travel outside Europe, by boat or otherwise, without medical insurance.

A final tip: many yacht clubs have a code of crewing practice, which may or may not cover financial and insurance issues. If your club has one, read it and abide by it.

I have learned that in life there are two possible ways to go, the way of resistance or the way of acceptance. This applies to everything in your life including sailing and financial agreements. If you want to have smooth passages and maintain your friendships it's a good idea to embrace the way of acceptance, for if you opt to follow the way of resistance, your life will be fraught with difficulties. It's as simple as that.

What I'm trying to convey is that arguing over money can be very unpleasant and can ruin an otherwise joyful expedition. Boating can be done on a shoestring, it can be a very costly exercise, or it can be anywhere in between. Work out for yourself what level of expense suits you and find sailing companions who are on a similar level. That's one of the key ingredients for a happy ship.

CHAPTER FIVE

BUILDING CONFIDENCE THROUGH TRAINING

Training in any field of endeavour is the fast track to building confidence, knowledge and understanding in the discipline in question so naturally sail training will add a lot to your enjoyment, safety and competence in sailing too. Quite simply, sail training makes you more capable and confident more quickly, so once you have shown yourself willing on someone's boat and decided you want to further your adventures afloat, now is the time to prove how motivated you are by going to a sea school.

In the UK, training even for skippers is not mandatory if you want to put to sea in a yacht on an amateur basis, but on a boat your life can depend on knowing what you are doing, or at least knowing what you ought to be doing. You may think this only applies to the skipper because he will tell everyone else what they need to do or know, and there is an element of truth in this – but only an element. It's not the whole truth. On a boat you really don't want to be dependent on anyone else for your well-being because occasionally something happens in the heat of the moment and you might need to react quickly on your own initiative.

As I described in a previous chapter, it's not unknown for you to find yourself at sea in the company of a skipper who is incompetent, or one who's good at skippering but not at teaching. It's also possible that the skipper falls overboard or has a heart attack – these things can and do happen, and there might not be time or opportunity to ask for guidance. Therefore the more you broaden and deepen your understanding and competence regarding every aspect of sailing, the better off you will be. What's more, you reduce the teaching burden on the skipper.

In any adventure sport there are risks and you have to accept that fact. The secret to a long and happy sailing "career" is to minimise that risk as much as possible by stacking the odds as much as you can in your favour so there is less likelihood of having a mishap. To do that, you need knowledge and experience. You can spend ages learning from your fellows "on the job," as it were, or you can speed up the process immensely by getting trained. There will still be plenty of "on the job" experience required as well, for you need to put into practise what you have learned. It's just like riding a bicycle, although a lot more complicated!

Having said that, the other important benefit of proper training is that your enjoyment is very much heightened as you begin to feel competent and confident around boats. Learning to sail involves a steep learning curve and the sooner you get to grips with the challenge the better for you and your fellow sailors. That way you begin to feel a part of something rather than just a spare part.

I sailed dinghies on a reservoir for a couple of years before I signed up for my first ever yacht trip, an RYA Competent Crew Course in the Solent lasting five days on a sailing school yacht (a Beneteau 36) with a professional instructor/skipper and three other students. Through dinghy sailing I had learned the basic principles of conducting a vessel under sail, for I had no engine on my dinghies, but I knew nothing of tides or navigation and little meteorology. I didn't need to; on a small lake with an island in the middle, it's quite hard to get lost, and there are no tides!

As per the joining instructions I joined the yacht for my Comp. Crew Course on a sunny Monday morning in a marina on Hayling Island, which, as you may be aware, is within the beautiful confines of Chichester Harbour. I was so excited I could hardly wait to get going, but the skipper and other students just sat around chatting and drinking coffee, talking incomprehensibly about something called the Chichester Bar.

I assumed Chichester Bar was a pub until I asked the skipper why we had to wait till lunchtime before we could set off. He explained that in fact it's a sand bar which our boat would be unable to cross until the tide had risen sufficiently to let our keel pass over it. That was my first lesson in tides. Though we were just sitting around drinking coffee I was already learning. That's the value of being in the company of a professional instructor and a crew who are eager to learn.

Everything is relative, and when you compare it to what the average boat owner is shelling out to maintain and sail his boat, not only does a course at a sailing school seem to cost remarkably little, but what you get for your money is a great bargain – the use of an expensive £40,000 plus yacht equipped and certified to a very high standard with which to try out and learn manoeuvres and techniques most skippers won't trust their crews with in a month of Sundays. Plus you get the loan or rental of expensive waterproofs and safety equipment, as well as expert tuition (I was soon to learn that the word BOAT is actually an acronym for Bung Over Another Thousand)!

Skippers cry out for people they can rely on, and even the most elementary course will propel you rapidly towards that objective.

People come to the UK from all over the world to participate in RYA (Royal Yachting Association) training courses because their training scheme is arguably the most highly respected one you can find anywhere in the world, so if you live in the UK, consider yourself blessed, though there are RYA accredited sailing schools in other parts of the world too. Further details about the RYA Sail Training Scheme can be found on their website, which is: http://www.rya.org.uk

The thing that really bowled me over when we did eventually get going on my first ever yacht trip was the sheer amount of multi-tasking required of a skipper and/or helmsman on a yacht in the Solent. After the simplicity of sailing my Mirror dinghy around a non-tidal lake, this was awesome. It seemed like non-stop, frantic activity from beginning to end, and very confusing, and it was only on the last, or fifth, day that things began to fall into place in my mind.

For example I had never used a winch before and I had never deployed or retrieved an anchor, and I'd never used a marine engine either – pretty basic stuff for a yacht crew, so the whole exercise was a massive learning curve. That was the whole point, of course. I learned how to use a winch safely without endangering my fingers, I learned to keep my legs and feet out of the way when laying an anchor chain and I learned how to do the daily checks on a marine diesel engine and to use it without crashing the gearbox or getting a rope around the propeller. I uncovered the mysteries of the marine toilet and for the first time in my life I did some night sailing – and lots of other things too numerous to mention.

At the end of the course I was given a certificate alleging that I was "competent" to act as crew on a yacht. But in truth I didn't feel in the least bit competent. I was only just beginning to get my head around what I'd learned and I felt I needed more practice to make it sink in and become second nature.

For that reason, shortly afterwards I signed on for another course with a different sailing school, this time a seven day trip from the Hamble River across to Cherbourg, the part of France nearest to the Solent and a favourite haunt of British yachties, then around the Channel Islands and back to the Hamble.

I told the skipper I didn't want a certificate, I'd already got that, I simply wanted more experience and practice, and trust me I got plenty. But more significantly, this was the trip during which I begun to understand the problems that can arise between people who are thrust together on a small boat (this time I was aboard a 35 foot Sigma).

We were six men, all British except one guy who was German. He was flying over from Germany to join us but he was to be a day late, and that irritated us before he arrived. Nevertheless we all tried to muck in as best we could.

Then one evening when we'd been circumnavigating some of the Channel Islands we moored up in St Peter Port, Guernsey and went ashore for fish and chips, which we brought back to eat on the boat.

We had a few beers to wash it down (just a few) and it was quite a merry evening until Hans, our German shipmate, clearly a little the worse from too much alcohol, brought up the subject of the Second World War. The rest of us immediately realised this could be a highly sensitive subject and fell silent, instinctively feeling the need to tread warily. Then Hans started telling us that Hitler had really been quite a good fellow at heart, and much misunderstood, allegedly. He told us that Hitler had actually been well meaning, and he'd done a lot of great things for Germany.

I could hardly believe my ears. To me this was like a red rag to a bull, especially because distant members of my family had suffered a very unpleasant fate in the Holocaust, and I could feel my face flushing red with anger. I could not help taking this personally and I was just about to explode in protest when the skipper caught my eye and gave me a look as if to say, "I'll deal with this." So I bit my lip and tried to maintain a dignified silence while the skipper skilfully changed the subject.

He was obviously far more experienced than I was in the difficulties that can arise between people on a boat and how to deal with them, and as a professional it was his job to make sure everyone had a good time, so he wasn't going to challenge anybody about their personal beliefs if he didn't have to.

The immediate situation had been diffused but relations on the boat never felt quite right again. The moral of the story –

if you want to be invited back to crew again another time, be very careful of talking insensitively about anything political, religious or highly emotive, and especially when it involves situations in which thousands of families had been wiped out or had their lives ruined.

But that wasn't the only problem. There was another fellow on the boat, a highly educated, nervous, insecure type, and his addiction was to be teacher's pet. As soon as the skipper asked someone to do something, he had to be the first one there doing it instantly, even if that meant pushing you out of the way. And when the skipper's back was turned he would try to bark orders to the rest of us, as if for some reason he was higher in the pecking order.

This caused terrific resentment among the rest of us – you could feel it in the air – and even the skipper looked as if he wanted to cringe. We'd all paid our money, we all had an equal right to be there and the only person in a position of seniority was the skipper. In the end we just ignored the irritating man, but the atmosphere on board was definitely unpleasant around him.

I made a mental note to myself that if ever I owned a yacht, or chartered one as skipper, I would never in a million years invite him to join my crew, even if he was the greatest sailor in the world, and that's the point I'm trying to get across. Trying to ingratiate yourself with the skipper, especially at the expense of the others, is a recipe for disaster.

If you sign up to do a training course with a sailing school, do what I did – focus only on learning as much about sailing as you possibly can and nothing else. That will always stand you in good stead and you will most certainly get your money's worth.

CHAPTER SIX

BUILDING EXPERIENCE –
THE CHARTER ROUTE

Experience is an invaluable quality and one that cannot be taught. In that respect, sailing is exactly like playing a musical instrument or learning carpentry in that you have to keep doing it time and time again, hands on, before you can hope to master the basic skills. Moreover, it is only when you reach that stage of getting the basic techniques firmly under your belt so you perform everyday routines almost on autopilot that you can really begin to relax and enjoy your sailing.

But if you don't have a yacht and you don't want to rely continually on friends to take you out in their boats, how can you do that? One way is by chartering a boat with friends, either in home waters or abroad.

Just one thing to bear in mind. If you are trying to build up the mileage in your personal log book to become eligible to take a more advanced skipper's course, your sailing has to be done in tidal waters or the miles won't count. If mile-building is your goal, the Mediterranean might not be the best place, nor parts of the Caribbean. Check the rules with the RYA before you decide.

As with everything in life there are pros and cons to chartering. It can offer many advantages, but to the unwary and inexperienced there can be pitfalls. There are also some legal niceties that must be observed. By relating some of my own experiences and lessons learned to illustrate these points, my hope is that you will have a happier and more joyful, trouble-free experience should you opt to go down the charter route.

There are three basic types of charter – *bareboat charter,* in which you get the boat to yourselves and one of your group acts as skipper, and *skippered charter,* which as the name implies, means you get a boat with a professional skipper who may also be an instructor, and you and your group acts as crew. At the highest levels you can charter a boat with a professional skipper and crew, and you and your group become passengers, though in some cases you can participate too.

If you are not confident that you and your group can cope, you could alternatively sign up for a flotilla holiday, in which a group of boats sail in company with a professional skipper on the lead boat.

For bareboat charter the person who will act as skipper will almost certainly be required to have an RYA Day Skipper certificate or higher. The qualification is more advanced than Competent Crew and is designed to introduce you to the art of skippering at a basic level. If chartering abroad you may also need a Helmsman's Certificate of Competence, also available from the RYA, because there are some countries, such as France, that do not recognise the RYA qualifications.

Also, you absolutely must have insurance – the charter company will almost certainly sort out the boat insurance for you, but you may have to arrange your own personal, medical and travel insurance. Make sure you read the small print if you don't want any nasty surprises.

My first bareboat charter experience was in the Greek Cyclades Islands and the boat we chose was an Atlantic 49 called *Zemini*, about five years old at that time. I organised the trip with a group of nine friends from my sailing club.

We arrived at the quayside in Athens and found the boat and the Greek charter company, who welcomed us aboard. Before signing the charter contract I said I wanted to inspect the boat and be shown how everything works. Well actually to be more accurate I should say how everything was supposed to work.

A young lad ushered me aboard and he immediately flicked on all the switches on the control panel by the chart table. Then we went out on deck and looked at the lights. The red navigation light on the port side of the pulpit wasn't working and when I pointed this out to the lad he stared at it for a moment, shrugged and then hit the pulpit with all his might. As if by magic, the light came on.

He looked at me with a triumphant smile as if to say, "job done!"

I remonstrated with him, saying that it wasn't properly mended and could fail again at any time. He spoke not a word of English, nor I a word of Greek, but he got my gist and immediately pulled out a roll of black insulating tape from his pocket and wound some tape around the pulpit over the cable where it emerged from inside the stainless steel tube. Now that he was completely satisfied there was no longer a problem he resolutely and implacably moved on to show me how the electric windlass worked. To my surprise it functioned perfectly.

Eventually we signed on the dotted line and summoned the courage to slip our lines and leave the dock. This boat seemed gigantic to me, being almost twice the length of the little 26 foot wooden boat I had by this time acquired, and I was mightily relieved that I didn't have to bring her stern-to a concrete quayside when we stopped later that evening, for on our first night we rested at anchor.

I'd been skippering my own little boat for a few years now, but I was still relatively inexperienced and I'd never had a boat with a roller furling genoa. The first time we let it out the wind caught it and pulled it out much too fast and later, when the wind piped up and we wanted to roll some of it back in we discovered that the furling line was jammed on the drum. We considered letting go the halyard, but the thought of the massive sail tumbling down onto the foredeck and thrashing around like a tortured animal while we fought and struggled to get it under control didn't really appeal.

Then I remembered an article I'd read in one of the yachting magazines in which someone had had the same problem and described how he solved it. First we started the engine to have it idling on standby in neutral and then I went down into the galley to find a sharp knife.

Jumping onto the foredeck I untied the lazy genoa sheet from the clew of the sail and then, standing well back, sliced through the one that was under tension. Immediately the giant piece of canvas flew out to leeward and while someone secured the furling line so that the drum at the foot of the furling gear could not rotate, we sheeted the mainsail in hard, put the engine in gear and drove the boat slowly round and round in circles until the sail wound itself around the forestay. It worked! All we had to do then was to tie a rope around it to stop it unrolling, drop the mainsail and motor calmly to our chosen anchoring spot, where we spent a relatively peaceful night.

In the morning we contacted the charter company who sent their local agent to sort us out. He arrived in a tiny rowing boat, took the sail down, freed the jammed furling line which was no longer under tension, re-hoisted the sail, furled it and re-attached the severed sheet to the clew of the sail.

This had been a feat requiring considerable strength, speed and agility and he was only a little bloke. But he had bulging muscles so naturally we called him Hercules.

Next day we were sailing merrily along when someone noticed there was a lot of water in the bilges. No problem, we thought, just switch on the two electric bilge pumps.

But after a while we realised that the forward section of the bilge was emptying nicely but the aft section was not. It was obvious that the aft pump was not functioning properly, even though we could hear the motor working, so we switched it off and started bailing. The only bucket we could find was so small it was going to take forever, so someone had the bright idea of using the kitchen waste bin, which was quite large, but had no handle.

We set up a system whereby one person sitting on the cabin floor next to the open bilge would submerge the waste bin and stand it up full while another person stood by to pass the now heavy vessel up to the cockpit where it was received by someone else who passed it to another person sitting near the side deck.

The last person in the chain then had the job of emptying the bin over the side of the boat before passing it back, now empty, so the process could be repeated over and over. Unfortunately, when the bilge was still about half full, the person charged with emptying the bin dropped it over the side.

"Bin overboard!" someone yelled, while the helmsman immediately headed up to windward to stop the boat. With that the foresail was promptly furled and someone put the engine on. Then we dropped the mainsail and motored back to the semi-submerged bin that we could clearly see bobbing on the waves.

Several times one of us grabbed hold of the distressed bin but it was so heavy and difficult to grip, try as we might we simply could not retrieve it. In the end we abandoned it, another addition to the detritus that floats around in the Med.

That night we came into a harbour and phoned the charter company again. This time we were in a different island, so there was no prospect of Hercules coming to our rescue. However, in the morning another young man came to find us and he took the pump away to be fixed. A few hours later he returned with the now functioning bilge pump. It had been blocked, that's all that was wrong with it. Another lesson learned.

That's when I also learned never to go to sea without a set of tools. With tools we could have fixed it ourselves in less than ten minutes while underway, and we'd never have lost our garbage bin, if only we'd been able open it up to find out what was wrong.

In this way we spent the first week of our fortnight's holiday fixing the boat as we hopped from island to island –

in effect doing the charter company's job for them, for it was obvious the maintenance on this boat was minimal, and that's being generous.

Lesson learned – in certain parts of the world the attitude to proper boat maintenance is cavalier to say the least, so don't go for a cheap deal like we did. Go to a reputable charter company and find out about their track record before you commit.

A couple of years later I decided to try again, this time with a boat that was only a couple of years old, based in Martinique, in the Grenadine islands of the Caribbean. Unfortunately, although I had learned one lesson and chose a much younger boat, I had not yet acknowledged that ten people on a fifty foot yacht is too many, even though there were ten berths. We wanted to keep the cost down, so we filled her to capacity.

She was a Dufour fifty, a lovely, powerful boat in much better condition than *Zemini* had been, except for one deck hatch that leaked when it rained straight onto my bunk. This meant I had to put up with a partially soggy mattress a lot of the time. Her name *Rhea* puzzled me for a long time, but later I found out that Rhea was the mother of the Titan gods, a symbol of female fertility, motherhood and generation. Her name also means "flow" and "ease". I also discovered that the Rhea is a flightless bird related to the ostrich, though quite why anyone would want to name a boat after one of those remains an enigma.

We thought we'd been very careful to book our holiday for well after the end of the hurricane season in the Caribbean but, as luck would have it, a powerful hurricane struck the region just a day or two before our intended departure from Heathrow. The upshot of this was that Antigua, the airport into which we were supposed to fly, was flattened and therefore closed.

So we waited 12 hours in a hotel at Heathrow while the former Beewee airlines decided what to do with us and thousands of other frustrated would-be holiday makers.

Finally we boarded a plane to Trinidad. We were relieved. Our boat was actually in Martinique and we'd heard from the holiday company she was unscathed. It was just a matter of getting there. Well, we thought, how hard could it be? At least we'd be on the right side of the Atlantic.

To cut a long story short we finally arrived at the quayside in Martinique after a completely insane journey from Trinidad in a series of tiny propeller driven ten and twelve seater planes, and nightmare drives in two high performance transit vans driven by a pair of crazy brothers who were clearly ardent fans of Formula 1, right across St Lucia from one airport to another, and off we went into the wild blue yonder aboard the good ship *Rhea*.

What followed was one of the best holidays I've ever had in my life, but it was not without its difficulties. Mostly it was problems between people again.

Just one of those problems was nothing to do with human relations but was due to the fact that in many of the places we visited, the shore facilities were wiped out by the hurricane, so instead of pulling into a bay to tie up at a jetty, as the pilot book said we could, there was no jetty, just a pile of matchwood stacked up on the beach. This made it very difficult to fill our fresh water tanks because instead of tying up alongside where there should have been a hose point, we were obliged to anchor off, being very careful not to damage the coral. Also, as with *Zemini*, our boat in the Greek islands, the outboard motor for the dinghy very rarely worked, so we got a lot of excise rowing.

As well as streaming an anchor from the bow, we were also advised to tie a line from our stern to a tree on the beach to hold us steady just beyond the surf line, but none of our ropes was anywhere near long enough. In the end we took every rope we could find, including the mainsheet and the two genoa sheets, and tied them all together end-to-end to make one very long line.

When we were in St Vincent, we discovered that the former beach café, now just a lump of twisted metal, concrete and broken glass, still had a functioning tap and a very long hose and one young man who had a rowing boat actually rowed the end of the hose out to our boat so we could fill our tanks. It must have been at least 100 meters long.

Food we were able to row out to the boat in our rubber dinghy and in some places we had to fill the tanks from bottles of mineral water that we bought ashore. We had a meeting and I as skipper again explained very carefully and clearly that water was at a premium and we must treat it as a valuable resource which had to be conserved and used sparingly. That meant, go for a dip in the sea if you need a wash and if you must have an occasional shower on board, be very frugal with the water. To me this was obvious and plain common sense, but for the benefit of our less experienced crew members, I decided to spell it out for them.

Now this is the kind of test I'm talking about. Imagine you are a crew member on this boat in the situation I have described. Will you be considerate to your fellow crew members by being careful with water, or will you selfishly use more than you need? Will you adapt to the unexpected circumstances and enjoy your sailing trip anyway, or will you constantly complain? You'll be amazed at the number of aspiring crew members who can't seem to cope with these simplest of demands. Such people do not get invited to come again a second time because, quite simply, they spoil the holiday for everyone.

One more anecdote which I hope will drive this message home: As the days went by on this same holiday I kept looking at the water gauge and wondering why the level was going down much more quickly than I was expecting. It was only some weeks later, back home in England, that I discovered that one of our crew members, a young, gung-ho sort of person who shall remain nameless but who was always stirring up trouble through a sort of covert resistance to doing what he had agreed to do, had been having three showers a day on board!

It was lucky he wasn't around when I found this out because I was so angry I felt I could have throttled him with my bare hands!

When you flagrantly disregard the skipper's explicit instruction or behave in manipulative ways designed to sabotage or undermine the skipper's authority, especially behind his back, do not expect another invitation. Ever! Be warned, the skipper will always find out eventually.

CHAPTER SEVEN

OTHER TYPES OF CHARTER

As one who loves to try different things I had an idea it might be an interesting experience to go sailing on some kind of tall ship or square rigged vessel, and eventually my researches led me to a brigantine named *Jean de la Lune* that used to offer skippered charter trips around the Western Isles of Scotland.

Once again I collected a merry group from my sailing club, this time we were twelve people but on a much larger vessel than *Zemini* or *Rhea*, and off we went, flying from London to Glasgow and then a drive in a coach that I had hired to join the vessel in Oban on Scotland's west coast. From there we enjoyed a delightful sailing trip around the Inner Hebrides, stopping at the much fabled islands of Muck, Eigg, Rum, Canna, and Tobermorey on the Island of Mull, as well as one or two places on the mainland, and passing Ardnamurchan point, a name familiar to those of us of a certain age from the shipping forecast on BBC Radio Four.

This was a chance for me to actually have a holiday for I was not skippering and I was quite relieved I didn't have the job of licking this motley crew into shape.

Our jolly ship had two masts, the foremast carrying three square rigged sails. Aft of that, the main mast, a little taller than the foremast, carried a fore and aft-rigged gaff mainsail and two large triangular stay sails in front of it. There was also a long bowsprit which carried two or three triangular foresails of varying sizes. Compared to the modern yachts I'd been sailing up till now, the brigantine seemed a bit of a cumbersome rig, not very happy when progressing to windward (almost impossible without the engine) but quite spritely with a stiff breeze abaft the beam.

This meant that because we had specific destinations in mind, we spent a lot of time motoring with only the fore and aft sails hoisted.

In case you might be interested, in its day (late 17th and early 18th centuries) the brigantine configuration was very popular, being one of the fastest and most manoeuvrable rigs of its era, and was thus much used for piracy, espionage and reconnaissance, or for supply and landing purposes in a fleet.

Jean de la Lune, atypically, was built in Brittany in 1957 and was one of the very last working sailing vessels built without an engine (she has one now). The hull is some 110 ft in length, with a long bowsprit, and she carries the classic brigantine rig as I described.

We were told by our skipper we were all welcome to climb the rigging on the foremast should we feel the urge, and our professional first mate showed us how. A friend of mine who'd spent ten years as a paratrooper in the Israeli army told me this could be his opportunity to conquer his fear of heights. "How can you have a fear of heights," I asked him, "if you were a paratrooper?"

"That's when I discovered I had a fear of heights," he replied. "They had to push me out of the plane."

He then suggested I should have a go.

"I have no need, no desire, and no motivation whatsoever to conquer my fear of heights," I assured him. "I'm perfectly happy to live with it. I'll stand on deck and shout encouragement to you."

He climbed the rigging and when he came down again he was ashen faced and I could hear his knees knocking. He had certainly experienced his fear of heights but I don't believe he'd conquered it!

This trip was a very unusual crewing experience. The boat was incredibly labour-intensive. To set or furl the square sails, which we only did once, several people had to not only climb the rigging but also to walk out along a rope slung under each yard to untie the sails and let them drop down, or to gather and tie them up when they became surplus to requirements. It took an entire morning to lower and set the three square sails and then furl them again, by which time those members of our crew who had completed the task were absolutely exhausted. This would require practice if we were to become accomplished, we realised.

On the plus side, the boat was huge and comfortable compared to what I was used to, the captain's wife, our chef, cooked up a storm, and we visited some stunningly beautiful places. What's more, once the wind got going and she started shifting, the feeling of sheer power was awesome.

I also learned a lot about how a crew can work together like a well-oiled military machine when the skipper gets everyone galvanised. There's a lot of satisfaction in being a part of that. A good crew member on a ship like this must be a team player and has to work efficiently and be committed. If the same ethos can be translated to sailing in conventional yachts, you have the perfect recipe for a happy ship.

While we were on board the skipper spoke to us about the possibility of organising another trip to visit some of the remote and wilder Outer Hebrides islands, but this, he explained, was a much further distance into very exposed waters and therefore required plenty of time and a stable weather window that would last several days, a bit of a tall order for that part of the world.

Being a glass half-full bunch of people, accordingly some of us signed up to come again the following year, but unfortunately the skipper had injured his back and was in severe pain most of the time, and the weather was not playing ball. So this time we mostly motored from one nearby island to another staying in sheltered waters, and we had a lot of time ashore while the skipper rested his back on board.

It was disappointing, but one of the first lessons a novice crew has to learn is that unless your skipper is very gung-ho, on a cruising boat you will spend a lot of time waiting for good weather, especially somewhere like Scotland where some areas are very exposed and the weather can be quite dramatic, but also even in places like the Caribbean. You just have to accept it and always bring a good book. "Me and my big ideas," I thought to myself ...

A couple of years later I read an article in *Practical Boat Owner* magazine about traditional barge sailing in Holland. This really looked like fun.

When I looked into it I discovered that the Dutch have got the whole scenario organised to a tee and it's a popular thing that attracts people from all over Europe and America, even non-sailors looking for an unusual holiday experience, or companies seeking a corporate outing. The barges were handled by specialist charter companies and everything was to a very high standard. You have to take a licensed professional skipper and first mate, but a cook was optional – these boats are not available for bareboat charter and after a couple of days on board I could understand why.

When making the booking, following our previous experience, I underlined that we were a group from a sailing club and we love sailing rather than motoring and for that reason the choice of skipper was as important as the choice of boat.

We were given the most wonderful skipper, a guy with a reputation for not liking to use his engine unless strictly necessary, and he certainly lived up to that. *Alida*, also a vessel over 100 ft long, was a two masted Rhine Barge (Rijnaak). The mainsail was gaff rigged and the mizzen similarly so. There was a long bowsprit on which up to three foresails could be set.

Below, the massive hold had been converted into a huge dining area, a large kitchen and twelve twin cabins, all with running hot and cold water. There were also several showers and toilets. Originally these boats were designed for carrying cargo, so the interior volume was vast.

Handling this boat required the utmost skill and judgement, as I discovered when I was handed the helm.

After a short time I was told to turn to starboard and I started to crank the large heavy wheel over. It took almost a whole minute.

I looked over the stern and I could see the rudder was hard over, yet the boat carried straight on. After what seemed like an eternity, she finally began to turn, at which time the skipper told me to turn the wheel fully over to port. This was most disconcerting because the boat was still turning to starboard.

Eventually, with the rudder turned the "wrong" way, the turning slowed and I brought the wheel and rudder amidships. Finally the huge lumbering beast settled into a straight line on her new course.

There were more fun and games when it came to hoisting the mainsail, which was made of a thick, heavy canvass material with a heavy gaff (spar) along the top of it. It took at least three of us to hoist it, using the biggest winch I have ever seen on a boat. We took turns on the giant handle, each of us hoisting the sail a few feet up the mast before moving over exhausted to allow the next person to grasp the handle and rotate it to raise it a few more feet. Most days it took almost ten minutes just get the mainsail fully hoisted.

The boom was also very long, which meant that the mainsheet, which was a very heavy rope, seemed to go on for miles. Every time we gybed we had to pull it all the way in, wait patiently for the boat to turn her stern through the eye of the wind, and then rapidly let it all out again on the other side of the boat. It was very, very hard work and we were glad we'd hired the cook, for by the end of the day our appetites were massive – we were burning so many calories, especially in the rather cool weather. This way we were able to concentrate on sailing the boat rather than cooking, and then dive below at the end of the day for a hearty meal without having to wait.

It was a fascinating week as we sailed through the Ijsselmeer, passed through the lock into the Markermeer, Holland's two non-tidal seas, and then back into the

Ijsselmeer to pass through another lock into the Waddenzee, which is very tidal and very shallow and has shifting sandbanks. Several times we saw other barges that had gone aground while we zoomed past.

The boat had two lifting leeboards, one either side of the hull, instead of a keel, so the boat could navigate these shallow waters under sail, and the skipper showed me how he partially lowered the leeward one so, if it touched the bottom, it would bounce back up and warn him he was getting too near the shallows. "That's my high-tech echo sounder," he joked.

I learned a lot on this trip, again it was mostly about how a crew working as a team can cope with the massive forces of such a huge vessel, and in very confined waters. Those of you who have read the Erskine Childers classic, *The Riddle of the Sands*, will recognise many of the Friesian Islands we visited, which added to the fascination, and everywhere we went we met the most wonderful people you could ever wish to meet.

***

If you want to learn to be a competent, versatile crew member on any vessel, it pays to take every opportunity that comes your way to go sailing, unless you know that the skipper or his boat is a disaster. And if nothing seems to be happening, create you own opportunities by organising something yourself.

It's really helpful to try out all sorts of different, diverse and exciting sailing experiences like the ones I have described in the last two chapters, until you find out what you prefer. It will broaden your experience and understanding of the art of cruising under sail, increase your enjoyment and confidence, and generally augment your competence.

That's what will get you invited back time and again. You can be taught knowledge but you can't be taught experience. You just have to go out there and do it as much as you possibly can. Skippers especially love crew who demonstrate an eagerness to learn, and there is so much to learn in sailing. It's never the same two days in a row.

CHAPTER EIGHT

MOVING OUT OF YOUR COMFORT ZONE

In many ways anyone who goes to sea will be called upon to move considerably outside their psychological and maybe physical comfort zone at times, by which I mean that all who go sailing will be tested sooner or later and have to dig deep inside to find inner strengths and essential resources they probably did not know they had.

It is times like these that really sort out the excellent crew from the average or plain useless, and they are precious moments that give you your opportunity to assess (afterwards) just how much you really love sailing, how much you trust your skipper, how much you trust and believe in yourself, and just how deep your commitment is.

Be honest, will you rise to challenge, or will you wish you'd never left the pub?

The following stories from my own experience illustrate how various crew performed (or failed to perform) in trying circumstances, and the effect this had on me, the skipper, and thus their potential for being invited to come back to crew again another day.

In my early days of boat-owning and skippering I had a 26 ft wooden boat, a South Coast One Design (SCOD) designed by Charles Nicolson, called *Lorette*. She was the first boat I ever had with an inboard diesel engine, a little 10 horsepower Yanmar which proved to be utterly reliable except for one small fault. The impeller for the cooling water pump used to "go" about three or four times every season.

The first time I chose to cross the English Channel from Cowes to Cherbourg in *Lorette* I found this out the hard way.

I should perhaps mention at this point that my knowledge of engines at that time, especially diesel engines, could probably be written on the head of a pin. I did not even know there was an impeller, nor even a sea water pump for that matter. All I knew, as we approached the outer harbour entrance at Cherbourg, having started the engine and dropped the sails, was that the overheating alarm started sounding, which I realised meant I must switch off the engine immediately or risk seriously damaging it.

Having done that my immediate reaction was to hoist the sails again, which we quickly accomplished, to at least keep the boat underway and under control and not just drifting at the mercy of the tide. Then maybe I'd be able to sail into the outer harbour and then the inner harbour and finally the marina, though that idea seemed a bit risky with huge ferries manoeuvring and going in and out fairly frequently.

What else to do? The only alternative I could think of was to drop the anchor and wait for a passing yacht or powerboat to hail for a tow, but the water was so deep I doubted my anchor chain would be long enough.

It was at this point that one of my crew piped up. He was a farmer and used to tractors with diesel engines and after some careful examination of my little Yanmar he declared that not only was the engine cooled by seawater, but there was a pump that pushes the water around the engine which he had found by following the water intake pipe. "There's probably something wrong with the pump," he postulated. "Let's have a look."

Out came the tools, and while my one other crew sailed the boat around in wide circles to one side of the harbour entrance, we unscrewed the cover of the water pump and found inside a rubber paddlewheel, which I subsequently learned is called an impeller. In the middle of the impeller was a bronze collar with one flat side that fitted over a shaft inside the water pump, and this shaft was obviously supposed to drive the bronze collar and hence the paddlewheel around. Unfortunately the bond between the bronze collar and the rubber or neoprene impeller had broken down and the collar was turning without moving the blades of the paddlewheel. Hence we deduced the cooling seawater was not being circulated around the engine, and that was why it had overheated.

"Give me your spare impeller," he said to me.

"What spare impeller," I replied. I had no spare because I didn't know of its existence, let alone that I might have need of one. My previous boat had an inboard petrol engine and the least said about that the better, save that it had no impeller that I knew of, and the boat before that, my first ever seagoing yacht, had an ancient but very reliable outboard two stroke petrol motor.

In the end, at my crew's suggestion, I found some Araldite two part resin adhesive, and he glued the collar into the centre of the impeller, and held the assembly very carefully high over a gas flame on the cooker for a few moments to dry quickly (very dangerous and not recommended because the adhesive is highly inflammable) before finally putting the impeller back into the water pump and screwed the cover on.

It worked! We started the engine again, heading straight through the harbour entrance towards the marina, furling sails as we went, attaching mooring lines and hanging out fenders to prepare for berthing, and covered the four or so miles to the marina entrance. No sooner had I spotted an empty berth ahead than the overheating alarm went off again about 100 yards from the berth. The adhesive had failed right at the critical moment.

But no matter because nothing was going to stop me now. We were heading straight for the vacant finger pontoon and nothing was in the way, so I gave her a burst of speed and cut the engine again while we coasted into the berth. My very selfsame crew managed to grab a cleat on the pontoon with a boathook while my other crew lassoed another cleat with the bow line and hey presto, we were finally tied on!

That is the kind of crew every skipper wants – a resourceful person with knowledge the skipper does not have but might need in an emergency, a creative thinker primed for action and with an abundance of common sense. In fact I was so relieved he'd solved my problem that when we went ashore I bought him dinner! That doesn't happen very often.

Just to finish off the story, next morning I went ashore and found the Yanmar agent. He didn't have a spare impeller so we had to wait three days until one came from Japan. Now I always carry at least one spare on my boat, preferably even two or three, along with various other engine spares. Moreover, when I got home to London, I signed up to do the RYA Diesel Engine Maintenance course, which teaches basic engine maintenance, very simple repairs and make-do techniques to get you home.

Incidentally, I would recommend everyone who goes to sea to do that course, especially if engines are a mysterious subject to you. The engine on a boat is such an important item of equipment it always pays sooner or later to build a friendly relationship with it. You never know when the information you learn on a course can get you out of trouble, and a lot of the course content is designed to help you prevent problems before they occur.

My axiom remains, *the better prepared you and your boat are, the more enjoyable and trouble free your sailing experience will be.* This applies whether you are crew or skipper. You may not be able to control or influence the preparation of someone else's boat, but there's no excuse for not preparing yourself.

By contrast to the above experience, another time I was crossing the Channel in the opposite direction in the same boat, but with a different crew, and after a couple of hours a gale blew up. It was a following wind so we decided to carry on under a small working jib with no mainsail and we were making steady progress. I knew perfectly well we were aboard a good ship, *Lorette*, a boat well capable of weathering the boisterous sea, though we were getting rather wet.

As so often in a gale it was a beautiful sunny afternoon, but as evening drew in we started to feel a little chilly, so someone was sent below to fetch pullovers and waterproofs. At that point both my crew started feeling seasick and soon they both went below to crash out on their bunks. That was the last I saw of them till morning.

I'd already been on the helm for about four hours by the time night fell and didn't want to use the autopilot for fear that I might fall asleep on watch if I wasn't having to do something physical that required concentration. By midnight I was really tired and finding it hard to concentrate. The wind moderated for a while so I started the engine and motored gently with the working jib (this boat did not have a roller-furling headsail) as that was far easier than hoisting the main on my own in the middle of the night with no one to look after the helm.

By about three a.m. I was starting to hallucinate, imagining I was running over pedestrians as I sailed along what seemed to be a motorway and seeing wild horses galloping across my path in the inky black night. I was still getting slapped in the face by the occasional wave, which added to the miserable situation.

Finally I saw the light at St Catherine's point, the southern tip of the Isle of Wight, way off on my port bow, exactly where I wanted it to be, but it was so dark I could not see any horizon and I couldn't really tell where the sea ended and the land began, and therefore how far off the island I was as I began slowly to pass it. I knew I had to keep a respectable distance off to make sure I safely cleared Bembridge Ledge, an outlying rocky plateau extending from the eastern tip of the island, and this I achieved by observing other vessels coming towards me and making sure I passed well outside of them. At this time satellite navigation for yachts had only recently been introduced and I certainly didn't have such equipment.

I slowed down to make sure I didn't get too close to the Portsmouth shore before sunrise and then I felt something foul the propeller, though the engine kept going, just about. We were limping along like a wounded animal when dawn broke and found us among the Forts between the Isle of Wight and the entrance to Portsmouth Harbour. Perfect.

All the while my crew had been utterly useless, down below fast asleep. As always happens when almost home, one of them surfaced and came up on deck and believe it or not he was angry with me for making him seasick and getting him cold and wet. I was speechless and, as the sea was much calmer now and there wasn't much wind I asked him to go on deck to lower the working jib and raise the genoa because we needed extra power to get into the harbour against the ebbing tide, and the engine was barely able to push us along. This he did, though he was very resentful of being asked to actually do some work!

Finally we crawled up the small boat channel into the harbour, whereupon we lowered the genoa and prepared warps (ropes for tying the boat up) and fenders. I knew that the Camber Dock, just inside the harbour on the starboard side, had a slipway outside the harbour pilot's office, so we carefully tied the boat up there and waited for the tide to finish falling. I knew she'd be left standing on her keel on the concrete slipway, so we carefully positioned the fenders and leaned her slightly against the wall as she went down.

At low water we walked down the slip to find a black plastic bin liner wrapped around the propeller and the shaft where it passes through the cutlass bearing. Luckily I was able to get it off with a sharp knife and dispose of it properly ashore. I had been very lucky the engine was only partially disabled. Then I went ashore for a well-earned shower and saw in the mirror, with a shock, that my face was completely white, as if covered with chalk. It was actually salt and it soon washed off.

Needless to say, neither of these crew members were ever invited back to sail with me. It was enough that I'd been left alone on the helm all night, probably for about 12 hours. I can understand someone being seasick, but to blame the skipper and be angry that he got you wet and tired is crazy. It made me so angry I sent them home and moved the boat back to her moorings on the Isle of Wight on my own, after I'd rested, of course. It was a lovely day now, pretty calm sea, very light breeze, I made a flask of hot coffee before I set off to have in the cockpit and simply motored gently across the Solent to my home base relishing the peace and quiet and thoroughly enjoying my own space.

Most self-respecting cruising skippers will not ask a crew to do anything they would not do themselves – or would not have done when they were young and agile enough. But rest assured, it's not only crew who get challenged. All skippers will also have had to move out of their comfort zone at one time or another.

I reiterate, as a member of a yacht crew you have to be able to look after yourself to a reasonable extent and if you are prone to sea sickness, you must be able to do something about it, otherwise you can become incapacitated and actually a liability. In the next chapter we will examine the issue of seasickness in greater depth, because it's a big one!

A few years later I met a woman who was to become my sailing companion, partner and later my wife, and we decided to sell *Lorette*, pool our resources and buy a more comfortable, larger boat. We settled on a beautiful Centurion 32, a fibreglass boat which we called *Samadhi*, built by Henri Wauquiez in France.

We'd been on passage from the Solent to the West Country, bent on cruising the gorgeous coastline of Dorset, Devon and Cornwall, and we'd been dogged by unstable weather for much of the time. We were on our way back east across Lyme Bay when fog caused us to divert into Exmouth, where we spent an irritating night in the river tied to a buoy which insisted on knocking against the hull all night, right next to

73

my ear! A friend of ours, Mike, was on board as additional crew.

Next morning the forecast was predicting south westerly force six wind. A bit on the strong side but not so bad for such a great sea boat, though we knew we'd have to be extra careful because we'd be sailing along a lee shore. We decided to stick our nose out of the river to see what conditions were like and before we could say Jack Robinson we were reefing the mainsail and rolling up copious amounts of genoa and still belting along at 7.5 to 8.5 knots on a broad reach.

That's pretty fast for a 32 foot yacht, and it was exhilarating – until we got out into the bay and started experiencing the most enormous rolling waves approaching us from just abaft our beam.

It was a bright sunny day with a piercing blue sky and every time *Samadhi* rose to a crest we could see for miles. But when we dipped into a trough, the world went dark and all we could see was the next grey wall of water towering some four feet above our heads rolling relentlessly towards us, and then we'd be levitated again to the top of the world, or so it seemed. Luckily, only three waves broke over us, swamping the cockpit as if we were standing in a swimming pool almost up to our knees.

Fortunately, no water went below decks, though we had the lower washboard in place as a precaution, and only a couple of weeks earlier I'd cleaned out the cockpit drains. Nevertheless, it took a full two minutes or so for the cockpit to empty itself each time.

Mike and I took turns to helm while my partner went below with our dog to keep out of the way and to make sure our canine friend was safe, and this went on for about ten hours. We were aiming for Weymouth, which entailed rounding Portland Bill, a jagged outcrop of rocky cliff with a dangerous tidal race off its tip. Eventually we passed it at a large distance to make sure we cleared the race, keeping a careful eye on the huge lighthouse, which seemed about the size of a matchbox.

We were hungry, but no one was going to attempt cooking or even making a sandwich, and we were thirsty, but the idea of making tea of coffee was out of the question. Luckily we had plenty of bottles of mineral water, some of which we kept in the cockpit, so we were not in danger of dehydration.

Once we rounded the Bill, we altered course for Weymouth, which meant coming round onto a dead run with the wind behind us and the sails goosewinged. Now the boat started rolling and my partner started feeling sick. But she managed to control herself and we carried on. We didn't want to slow down because we wanted to get into the sanctuary of the harbour, and get past the opening bridge into the inner harbour and marina before it closed for the night. We wanted to be absolutely sure of a safe, secure and quiet berth for the night, and that's exactly what we achieved.

We were so hungry by this time we quickly tied the boat up, jumped ashore and within ten minutes we were ordering our meal in the Chinese restaurant, though I'm sure the room was going up and down. This has to go down in history as the scariest passage I have even made, and I was so grateful for the unfailing assistance of Mike, my illustrious crew.

In contrast to the previous story, Mike had behaved brilliantly and demonstrated some really solid helmsmanship. Helming is an essential skill that a crew needs to master and it requires concentration, even if you are having a conversation at the same time. In testing conditions when you can't afford to put a foot wrong for fear of causing damage or danger to the boat and/or the people on board, it requires even more intense concentration. Mike and I took turns doing that for hours.

Needless to say, Mike has an open invitation to come back any time he wants to join us.

CHAPTER NINE

THE PSYCHOLOGY OF SEASICKNESS

Now that we've seen many examples of great and hopeless crewing it seems like a good moment to discuss the perennial issue of seasickness.

I've said this many times yet most seasick sufferers poo poo my assertion, nevertheless I am convinced that unless you have some rare physical condition that makes it inevitable, you don't have to suffer from seasickness. You can get over it. It's easy to talk yourself into being seasick, but it's just as possible to talk yourself out of it, though I'm not saying the latter is easy. If you suffer from seasickness and you want to free yourself, it does require considerable focus, concentration and determination, at least in the beginning.

The good news is, although there are physical reasons for it, being seasick is a state of mind, and you can always change your state of mind.

It's not just me saying this. I have discovered quite a lot of research into this subject, most of which seems to back up my assertion by and large, as you will see if you read on.

I'm not a psychologist but I am the son of a hypnotherapist and the husband of a psychotherapist and I have been around long enough to trust my own experiences and observations both of myself and of the many and varied people I have sailed with, anecdotal though these may be. Moreover I've seen it time and time again with clients in my Life Coaching practice, as well as when sailing. If you set yourself a goal and you seriously *desire* to achieve it, you have to consciously make a sincere decision deep in your heart that you will do it and be successful. Once you've made that commitment to yourself, you're already half way there and the rest is just a matter of procedure – meaning you simply take whatever steps you have to take to achieve your goal.

Even better, you *act as if* you have already achieved it. The achievement is already done and dusted, it's a foregone conclusion. Your self-belief then makes the achievement inevitable. In other words, you act as if you feel fine and eventually the time will come when you don't have to act any more.

What's more, once you've made up your mind in this way and set fire to that yearning desire to feel well on board at all times, the first steps you need to take will become self evident to you. It's like giving up smoking.

Every significant achievement begins with a burning desire. You really have to want the desired outcome. In this case, the goal is to get over feeling sick at sea, but like any other goal, once you have made your heartfelt decision your resolve becomes unshakable.

It's crucial to understand that you do not necessarily need to know how you will achieve any goal before you commit to tackling it. What you need is an unshakable resolve and a positive mindset, and they will be enough to guide you towards taking your first step. It's also important to realise you can't just wish the sickness away, you must take action, even if that action is in your head.

In the previous chapter I mentioned that sooner or later everyone who goes to sea will be called upon to dig deeply inside themselves to find extra resources they probably didn't even know they had, and I also mentioned that "average" people never learn to sail. Well this is a classic example of what I'm talking about. I reiterate, if you want to develop into something more than just a passenger, you will have to venture outside your comfort zone sooner or later, probably more than once, and do something extraordinary.

This applies not only to seasickness but also to any disability that hampers your progress – you have to find ways to rise above it. And getting over seasickness is absolutely doable, just like getting over a fear of flying or getting off drugs or alcohol. The addiction may still be there in the background but it no longer ruins your life because you've decided to get over it and you've done whatever it took.

Professor Michael Stadler from the University of Bremer writes in his book, *The Psychology of Sailing*, "The most important triggering factor (in becoming seasick) is the fear of seasickness." That is not to say that seasickness is not caused by physical and neurological functions of the body – it clearly is, but as in virtually any condition you care to name, fear or anxiety make it far more likely to occur or get worse. Therefore, the answer is to do something to allay the anxiety or fear, perhaps by simply developing a positive attitude.

Stadler continues, "This kind of anticipatory fear of seasickness is learned or – in psychological terms – conditioned by one or more negative experiences in the past."

That could be as simple as believing you got seasick yesterday, therefore you'll get seasickness again today. Or even holding the belief, "I'm prone to seasickness." Neither of these is necessarily true, but as long as you cling to those self-limiting beliefs about yourself, it's almost certain to happen. On the contrary, if instead you say to yourself something like, "I'm determined to feel fine and enjoy our sailing today," and keep remembering that promise to yourself, especially at moments when you feel challenged, it's much more probable that you'll be alright.

So what does it take to get over seasickness?

Some people manage it with medication, for example seasickness tablets. Unfortunately these often make you sleepy, which means you're replacing one problem with another problem. My wife tried using Scopolamine patches –

you stick one behind your ear – but that made the pupil of the eye nearest to the patch go very small, which to me seemed quite alarming. You can't get them in the UK except I believe by prescription, so she used to buy them in the Channel Islands. They were effective on her and they didn't make her drowsy, but I would never feel qualified to recommend anything like that because it might have an adverse effect on the body.

Interestingly, one day we were out sailing and she ran out of patches, which led to her discovering she'd got over her seasickness naturally. Now she very rarely feels sick and she uses nothing. She just got out of the habit of feeling sick (please note the deliberate use of the word habit).

Some people need nothing other than two or three days to get used to the motion of the sea and the boat.

I've known several people who have tried wearing special wristbands each of which has a little button on the inside which lightly presses against an acupressure meridian on the underside of each wrist, and there seems to be a roughly 50/50 split between those who said it worked and those who said it didn't.

I've also come across two or three people who tried wearing a copper bracelet and one who wore a bracelet with magnets inside it, but I never found out the results. If you find something that works for you, fine, don't change a thing unless you are worried about possible deleterious medical side-effects.

Incidentally, as a skipper I would never put anyone who had taken the conventional seasickness medication on the helm or on watch, for fear that they might fall asleep. In fact I would encourage them to do just that – go below, lie down on your back and go to sleep.

Perhaps I am biased, but I am not convinced by any of these so-called solutions because I don't like to rely on drugs or devices to solve my problems. My life experience tells me that the power of the mind is what needs harnessing in such cases. You have to get your psychology right. I guess the secret is you have to be seriously motivated from your heart by your burning passion to enjoy your sailing if you want to properly crack these kinds of problems.

Many years ago I had a girlfriend who just had to look at a boat to start feeling queasy. At the time I had a tiny boat, my first ever yacht, and she was tied firmly to a pontoon (the boat, not the girlfriend) in a flat calm harbour when the lady in question first stepped on board. Next thing I knew she was in floods of tears because she was suddenly feeling really sick, trembling like a leaf and she'd turned as pale as a ghost, even though the only movement was a slight rocking when we stepped on board.

Then she started getting a violet migraine and had to go below to lie down. The boat was still tied to the pontoon and the water was still as flat as a pancake and there she remained motionless for three entire days, occasionally sitting up to sip a cup of hot, sweet tea, until she felt just about well enough to step ashore. We gave up any idea of going out boating and drove home to London.

I learned later she had a chronic fear of the sea and of course I immediately realised that she and I would never go sailing together. It may sound blindingly obvious, but if you decide to crew on a boat you have to actually want to go boating, and not just because your boyfriend or girlfriend wants you to. You have to be prepared to transcend any difficulties, and that was the last thing she wanted. That's fair enough, and if that turns out to be the case for you too, best to accept it and move on.

By contrast I have a friend from my sailing club who has a brilliant technique for dealing with this. Many times I have been on a boat with her and she's fine for a while and then suddenly she starts to feel sick. I can always tell because normally she's loquacious in the extreme, but when she starts feeling not so great she falls silent. She never does that ashore.

As soon as she starts feeling sick, she finds somewhere to sit down, rests her head in her hands and keeps still, usually gazing into the distance. Clearly something is going on inside her head because nine times out of ten she gradually starts talking again after about ten minutes, a clear signal that she's got over it.

There have been two or three occasions when the feeling came over her before she noticed and took action, and she had to lie down for a while in the cockpit. But I've never actually seen her be sick and when I've asked her to move so I could get to a winch or whatever, she was able to do so, meaning she was not completely incapacitated like many people are. It appears she managed to control her sickness by simply staying calm and silent and letting it pass.

This is an admirable quality which encourages skippers to invite her out on their boats again.

In actual fact the best solution is disarmingly simple – relax!

This might involve first consciously identifying what is making you anxious. For example, if you are concerned about how to use the ship's toilet but are too embarrassed to ask, you could get anxious unnecessarily. Just ask the skipper and he will quietly and politely demonstrate the use of the toilet, and if necessary show you again until you understand, and once you have got it and tried it a few times your anxiety is gone.

But often a person's fear or anxiety is more general or caused by something that doesn't have a ready solution, for example going to sea makes you nervous, or having to socialise at close quarters with a bunch of strangers for a few days feels daunting, or the fear you might not be "good enough" engulfs you, or you fear not being able to understand what you are being asked to do. There are many things that can make us anxious, some justifiable and some not. You might fall overboard and drown, that's something real to fear and you need to be aware of that. What I'm saying is that it might not be the actual fear of being seasick that makes you feel seasick, there could be other reasons for being anxious and therefore feeling queasy.

In that sort of situation you just have to accept that you have these fears and get on with it, because no amount of reassurance will help at least until you've had some positive experiences. That's why I suggest you relax.

Of course that might be easier said than done.

Professor Stadler says we need "a simple method ... for breaking down the learned or anticipatory fear ... One should talk oneself through a relaxation exercise ... A positive consequence of this is a partial or complete relaxation of the muscles which counteracts the feeling of anxiety and with it the incipient seasickness. With time one manages to induce a relaxed state relatively quickly so that, in an emergency, the symptoms of anxiety can be overcome in a short time."

When I started sailing, I made a firm promise to myself never to be seasick. There have been one or two occasions when I felt a bit queasy, usually when I was very tired, and my method is to immediately think about something else. If possible I try to keep still and look at the floor of the cockpit (or cabin if I'm below), but if I'm helming I look around and try to work out what another boat on the horizon is doing, or watch the antics of seagulls following a fishing boat or something like that, to engage in whatever is going on around me so I forget about how I'm feeling. It's very difficult, probably impossible, to have your attention focused on more than one thing at a time, just like it's impossible to smile and frown simultaneously, so in this way I simply choose to pay attention to anything other than feeling sick. On those rare occasions I have to do this, I find it essential also to keep calm and stop talking. In this way I begin to relax and immediately start feeling better.

Because I've been a Life Coach and a teacher of meditation for some years, as you may have gathered by now, I have developed many techniques and strategies for calming myself down and relaxing quickly. Also, when I was a child I was taught by my father how to do self-hypnosis and to understand the power of auto-suggestion. You can literally talk to your mind and tell it how you want it to be or what you want it to think about. To anyone who suffers from anxiety, let alone seasickness, I urge you to learn some relaxation techniques. They will always stand you in good stead, both aboard and ashore.

Sometimes I have to remind myself, "This seasickness doesn't belong to me. I don't want it. I refuse to have it," or "I don't want to have anything to do with seasickness," or "I feel fine," or even, "I don't believe in seasickness." Sometimes I cajole myself with comments like, "come on, get over it." Then the key for me at that point, as I said, is immediately to think about something else. Any of these might work for you too, or you might have to develop your own techniques or affirmations, but one way or another, it can be done – and then, goodbye to seasickness!

I learned most of these techniques when I was a child of about eight years old. My father, not only a hypnotherapist but also a general practitioner and originally a surgeon, used to give me anti-histamine tablets to "cure" my hay fever. But they made me feel drowsy and I didn't want to feel like that all through the summer, so one day I simply decided to get over it. I gave up taking the tablets and that was the last time I suffered from hay fever. I used the same technique at an even younger age to get over asthma. I simply decided I didn't want or need it any more. There was no way I was going to run around carrying an inhaler.

My dad said I grew out of it, but I distinctly remember on both occasions making a conscious decision and feeling absolutely determined. And it worked!

It's important to realise that just because you were seasick does not necessarily mean you are a hopeless landlubber, but if it keeps happening you have to do something about it before it becomes an issue. If you want to be a fully active participant, you can if you believe you can and you owe it to yourself to at least try. Sailing is supposed to be enjoyable but it's very easy to be put off by seemingly insurmountable difficulties. That need not happen to you if you are prepared to make an effort.

Another point to remember. Some people, when they start feeling sick, have a habit of lying down prostrate in the cockpit, motionless and incapacitated like a sack of potatoes. This is really annoying for everyone else because you are taking up at least two or three seating positions, which means everyone else is squashed. But the real problem is that it makes it far more difficult to move around the cockpit, which is almost always a confined space, so every time the others tack or gybe the boat, they have to overcome an immovable obstruction when handling the winches.

If you have to lie down, please go below out of the way. I know some people feel worse when they leave the fresh air of the cockpit, but once you are lying on a bunk you'll probably fall asleep and you won't notice the difference. Oh, and if you're on my boat, please don't lie down on the upholstery while still wearing your sopping wet waterproofs!

Also important, don't let yourself get cold. If you're feeling too ill to find your dry pullover, ask someone who feels well to get it for you. And if you get too hot, take it off. I've seen so many people compound their suffering unnecessarily by being embarrassed to ask for help.

Two final points. If you are in the cockpit or on deck and you think you might be sick, *do not lean over the side of the boat to be sick into the sea,* even if you are wearing a lifejacket and safety harness. When a person starts feeling ill they often also feel a bit wobbly, and leaning over the side of a moving boat is dangerous even at the best of times. Ask someone to fetch you a bucket and use that within the relatively safe confines of the cockpit or, even better, take it down below. By doing that, you'll save the skipper a great deal of anxiety, and everyone else too, and perhaps also prevent a man overboard situation.

Finally, please don't hog the toilet! If you've locked yourself into the only loo on the boat so you can be sick in private, I need hardly explain why this could prove extremely inconvenient and embarrassing to other crew members, including the skipper.

Don't let your problems become other people's problems – use the bucket!

Stop press

As I finish this chapter, something new has been brought to my attention, anti motion-sickness glasses and anti motion-sickness sunglasses.

They've obviously been around for a while because they seem to have been under hot debate on some on-line boating forums, where opinions seem to be divided. I've never tried them myself, nor do I know anyone who has, so all I can do is report that they exist and leave you to find out for yourself, if you feel motivated to do so.

According to the advertising, the glasses only need to be worn for a few minutes (six minutes on average) before symptoms of sea sickness disappear, and they can be worn over normal prescription glasses. They are available from most chandlers or on-line and at the time of writing cost between £50 and £60, well worth it if they work, in my opinion. There are several manufacturers.

Clinical tests allegedly carried out with the French Navy, claim to have shown them to be 95 per cent effective, which is generally much higher than other seasickness remedies, and because no medication or drugs are involved there are believed to be no side effects.

That said, I still firmly believe it's worth trying my psychological approach first, especially as learning to train you mind is an invaluable life skill that will always be useful.

CHAPTER TEN

BASIC ESSENTIALS

The right gear greatly increases your enjoyment and enhances your safety, and the converse is also true – the wrong gear, or lack of gear, ruins your enjoyment, makes you miserable and can compromise your safety.

Here we discuss the basic essentials for looking after yourself properly, such as what clothes to bring, what to do on board and what must be done ashore, what to eat, how to avoid dehydration, hypothermia and exposure, how to maintain energy levels, preparation, watch keeping, making sure you get enough sleep, avoiding exhaustion, and other essential topics.

It is said that in the British Isles it is not unusual to experience all four seasons in one day even in the summer! Accordingly, the well prepared crew will be ready for anything, whether he needs thermal underwear and a chunky pullover one minute or a pair of shorts and a bottle of sun tan lotion the next. If you are going abroad, make a point of finding out what climatic conditions to expect and prepare accordingly.

Also find out what, if any, vaccinations you need. You can do that by consulting your general practitioner and/or visiting www.nhs.uk. Protection from nasty illnesses is a surprisingly technical business and it's always a good idea to seek professional medical advice well in advance (at least six weeks) before going anywhere abroad.

It's always wise to have protection from Tetanus and possibly Rabies, even in the UK, and some popular international sailing destinations are high risk for Malaria, Hepatitis A and B, Yellow Fever and many other conditions too numerous to mention that you really don't want to experience.

The reason you must plan this well in advance is because some treatments have to begin several weeks before you leave the UK and some require repeat doses. This is a really important issue because an ill crew member is not only useless and a liability, but within the confines of a boat, catching some nasty lurgy, especially if it's contagious, could be an absolute disaster for the whole crew.

Make sure you have the necessary documents if going abroad. A valid passport is obviously essential, and for some countries you may need a visa. Travel insurance, which we have already covered, is also a must in my opinion. It's also a good idea to take your driving licence in case you arrive in a place where you want to hire a car or motorbike. And if you do hire a vehicle, make sure you take the insurance and *read the small print* before committing yourself. Also take with you any relevant details of medication you are on, and any medication to which you are allergic.

Also be aware that if, like my wife, you have had hips or other joints replaced, airport metal detectors will be set off by the titanium or other metals inside you, and therefore you need the required documentation to prove you've had this surgery done.

Finally, check in advance with your service provider that your mobile phone will work in the places you will be going to in case of emergency and don't forget to bring some means of charging it from the mains as well as from the boat's 12 volt DC supply. Always protect your phone from getting wet.

Bear in mind you may or may not be able to get a Wi-Fi connection, depending on where you are, but even at sea if you are within two or three miles of the coast in most places, you will probably get a mobile phone signal so you might be able to use the Internet as well as send and receive text messages and make phone calls.

Remember, skippers get irritated if they want to call upon you to do something and find that they can't communicate with you because you are buried in your phone, so before you use it, check with him that it's an appropriate moment. I always insist, when skippering, that all phones and other devices (especially mine) are turned off when performing critical manoeuvres, such as approaching or leaving a berth, hoisting and setting sails, and so forth.

Clothing

As far as clothing is concerned, layers are the key, and preferably breathable layers, for with layers you can easily adjust the level of protection you need from the elements to suit the weather conditions of the moment. This way you never need to be too cold or too hot, nor uncomfortably sweaty. Remember that in many warm climates it gets chilly at night, so you might want a pullover and jacket even for going ashore. There's nothing that ruins a great meal quicker than shivering on the terrace of a restaurant.

Thermal underwear, with long sleeves and long legs can be an absolute boon, and I would never go overnight on a boat without them, even in the height of summer, and especially in a European, Scandinavian or Baltic region. If you get too hot you can always change into conventional underwear.

As for mid layers trousers are obviously important and there are many different types. Sailing trousers that have reinforced knees and backside areas are excellent, but you can get something similar under the name of work wear from many builder's merchants, usually at a much more reasonable price.

Modern fabrics are a godsend, because they are light and amazingly effective. You can be dressed for the coldest weather without feeling like an overstuffed, trussed-up chicken, and you can move easily. I once found some fleece-lined trousers which were also reasonably waterproof and they were wonderful – I loved them. They were really comfy and cosy and very lightweight. The only problem was they rustled loudly when I walked around, and the outer surface was slippery. Slippery on a boat is not a good idea, but nevertheless, the aforementioned trousers saw me happily through many a cold and wet passage. If it's really very cold, you can wear them over your thermal long johns.

It's also essential to have various long-sleeved shirts, in fact I have a fleece shirt which is as light as a feather and ridiculously warm. A lightweight cotton shirt is great on a warm day when you want to keep covered from the sun, and one or two heavy duty shirts are also very useful. I once had one with a quilted lining which looked for all the world like a lumberjack's shirt and it was a boon on cold days.

If you're experiencing hot sunshine obviously you want some shorts, and I find a short-sleeved shirt far more comfortable than a tee shirt because the wind can blow though it to keep you cool, whereas a tee shirt tends to stick to you and usually gets horribly sweaty.

Do not underestimate the power of the sun, especially when you are near the sea and particularly on a boat, in which you spend a lot of time exposed to the elements. High factor sun tan cream or lotion or sun block is a must, but don't forget to use it! Sunburn is very unpleasant, so always keep a bottle of Calomine lotion on board, and don't forget the danger of melanoma.

I've noticed that people who live in hot countries almost invariably seek the shade, yet they still get a tan. I try to do likewise. When sailing it is sometimes possible to sit or stand in the shade of the mainsail, and boats that sail regularly in sunny places usually have a bimini (permanently rigged sunshade) over the cockpit. Take full advantage of these and if necessary in harbour rig some kind of makeshift sun shade.

If a tee shirt or vest with a shirt is not enough it's time for a pullover of some sort, or a deck coat or jacket, or both. I once made the mistake of signing up for a five day sailing course in the Solent in February, and even though I put on every item of clothing I had with me, including scarf, hat and gloves, by the third day the cold was starting to penetrate right through to my bones. It was also constantly raining and I became very miserable.

At the end of that day I realised I'd spent the latter part of the afternoon just sitting stock still in the cockpit, staring into space and taking no interest in anything, a sure sign of the early stages of hypothermia, though I didn't realise that at the time. Afterwards, thinking about it, I thought it a bit odd that no one else on board seemed to be affected, so maybe I'm not very resistant to the cold.

At the end of the day, as it was getting dark, we motor-sailed into Portsmouth harbour and tied the boat up in the Camber Dock, not twenty yards from the pub. In those days you had to climb up a vertical iron ladder set into the quay to get ashore. I suddenly came to life and as soon as we were tied up I was up that ladder and into the pub like a jackrabbit. I wasn't waiting for anybody!

Oh bliss, I was out of the rain and there was a roaring log fire in the corner. I just stood in front of that fire dripping puddles all over the carpet and refused to budge all evening. It was a full two hours before I would even unzip my heavy duty foul weather jacket. At last I began slowly to thaw.

It was a salutary experience and an extremely unpleasant one to boot, so much so that I resolved never to go sailing again in the winter in these latitudes. I've stuck to that for years because I learned that I personally can't cope with prolonged exposure to cold weather, on a boat or anywhere else for that matter.

If you are aspiring to become a regular crew, it's very important to know all about yourself in this way. If you get invited to sail in a situation where you might not be able to function or look after yourself properly, or you might get ill, it's best to politely turn down the invitation, but tell the skipper why so he doesn't think you are being rude or unappreciative. Skippers don't want someone on board who might become a burden, so he or she will be grateful for your honesty.

In any case, if you know you are going to miserable, what's the point?

I had a friend who was crewing on my boat once who began to exhibit similar symptoms to the ones I've described above, so I told him he should go below and put on his pullover, and stay below for a while to keep out of the weather. But he insisted he was fine even though he continued to sit in the aft corner of the cockpit all huddled up and trying not to shiver. I repeated my suggestion more strongly, but he still insisted on toughing it out.

I thought it was bravado but to my surprise as soon as we were tied up in harbour he went below and put on his pullover. I was puzzled that he'd waited this long and not done it way before and then suddenly I twigged. He feared that going below while we were underway might make him seasick and that was why he didn't want to do it, but of course he'd never admit to that.

I just quietly told him if that happened again, he should ask someone else to go below to fetch his pullover. We wouldn't have minded. But he just shrugged it off and made out everything was fine.

Why suffer just because of your pride, I thought to myself? It seemed to me that this was a grown adult behaving like a child. It's just plain daft to suffer unnecessarily. As I have said, no skipper wants to be your nanny. The problem would have been easily solved if he'd simply asked for assistance. There's no shame in taking responsibility for your problem by doing that. I wished I'd realised what was going on with this guy at the time, then I could have asked someone to get his pullover for him.

To return the subject of clothing, a proper set of waterproof foul weather gear is an essential investment. On a yacht, most people opt for separate trousers and jacket, which also gives you the essential added facility of large pockets, but you can get an all-in-one suit if you prefer, though this is less versatile and usually only used by dinghy sailors.

If it's rough you will very likely get wet, and if it rains, you will certainly get wet, so you need something, preferably breathable (meaning the fabric allows your sweat to evaporate out to the open air), that's up to the task. Even a short passage of ten miles can take three or more hours, which is plenty enough time to get you thoroughly wet or soggy if your gear is not up to scratch. Don't skimp on this – a good set of "wetties" will last for years if you look after it, and if you buy something substandard you will almost certainly regret it when it starts raining or getting rough.

Having said that, it is very easy to spend a small fortune on foul weather gear, and there's probably no need to go to extremes. The manufacturers tend to grade their clothing for coastal or inshore sailing, or for offshore or ocean sailing, and the cost increases correspondingly. I've never understood this concept as you can get just as wet, or even wetter, doing inshore sailing as you can when going blue water. Whatever you choose, make sure it's suitable for the kind of sailing you're doing.

Two features I would recommend are reinforced knee and backside patches on the trousers, and to ask the retailer or manufacturer if they are sure the garment is totally waterproof, not just shower proof or water resistant.

Footwear is a difficult subject and over the years I've experimented with many different kinds. Knee length sailing boots (not quite the same as wellies) are an option, but I gave up on those because they are so heavy and difficult to get on and off in a hurry, and I found them uncomfortable.

Ankle length sailing boots are another possibility, but when there's a lot of water coming on deck, it can find its way over the top of them and then you find you've got soggy, squelchy feet and the water can't get out unless you take them off. Emphatically not desirable.

I keep my boat in France nowadays and I never sail in winter, so most of the time it's quite warm or hot, even when it's wet. So I have taken to wearing Crocks, which are actually plastic shoes a bit like clogs or sandals, and they have holes in them. These I wear without socks so if my feet get wet it doesn't matter. Any water soon drains out and they are plastic so they don't mind getting wet, but obviously that only works in a warm climate. Most important, they don't seem to slip on a wet deck and they are comfortable. You can even go into the shower with them on if they need cleaning.

A good pair of leather deck shoes for fair weather sailing is *de rigueur* in my opinion. They are comfortable, long lasting, versatile and they even look good ashore.

Various things to remember about footwear on a boat: Never wear shoes that have leather soles and never ever go on board a boat with stiletto heels (nor any other kind of high heels) unless you want the skipper to have an apoplectic fit. Also, some shoes and boots that have rubber soles leave black marks on the deck which can be very hard to remove, so check your shoes or boots don't do that before you come on board, or you won't win any popularity contests.

I had a holiday on a Gullet in Turkey a couple of years ago and this vessel had the most magnificent teak decks. The skipper would not allow us to wear any shoes at all on deck – not even proper yachting shoes. We had to be barefoot, like it or not. We even had to carry our shoes ashore and put them on at the quayside. This gave rise to another problem, by midday when the sun was at its zenith, the decks were scorching! We soon learned to walk around the boat treading in the shady areas.

Most important of all, and this has to be a golden rule, you must make sure your footwear does not slip on any wet surface. If they do, they are potentially dangerous! Footwear that is specifically designed for sailing has specially cut soles made of a special rubber to make sure they don't slip.

In cold weather some sort of hat is invaluable because most of the heat loss from our bodies is through our scalp. Most people opt for the woolly hat that pulls over your head, with or without a bobble on top (the bobble is only important if you are a fashionista). Unless it's extremely cold I usually go for a baseball hat, because the peak keeps the sun out of my eyes and protects them from the glare reflected by the sea.

I once bough a fleece hat, in a golf shop actually, and that is very effective. In fact sometimes it's too hot and it feels as if my brain is being slowly roasted so I have to take it off!

Gloves can be a problem. Typical crewing gloves that you find in any chandler are usually of the fingerless variety, which I find a bit useless because while my hand is nice and warm, the tips of my fingers are going blue. They are usually made of something that looks like suede or chamois leather to make sure they grip ropes, a tiller or a steering wheel.

Conventional woolly gloves are not much use either because they slip or feel cumbersome, and when they get wet they feel horrible, and conventional leather or plastic gloves are also not suitable because they also feel cumbersome and not sufficiently flexible.

I solved this problem when I was once in a camping and hiking shop where I found a pair of gloves made of something called Thinsulate, which is a very fine and light synthetic fleece material. The gloves completely enclose your entire hand, they are adjustable and you can even tighten up the cuffs with a Velcro strip to keep the water out. Although the material in fairly thin, inside the gloves your hands are as warm as toast and you can perform most manual boating tasks with them on. They also seem to be pretty waterproof.

Finally, if it's blowing hard and a bit chilly I usually wear a conventional scarf to make sure I don't get a sore throat.

The only other thing you might want is a change of clothing in which to go ashore.

So that's got clothing covered, although I realise I haven't said anything specific about women's clothes. That, to be honest, is because I don't feel qualified to do so. Nevertheless, exactly the same principles apply, and in any case most of the women I see around me wear trousers or shorts for sailing. As for more intimate items of apparel, forgive me but I'm not going to go there.

Now the perennial problem of what to put the clothes in to bring them to and from the boat. The golden rule here is never bring a suitcase on board a boat, for the simple reason, unless it's a huge mega-yacht there will be nowhere to stow it, which means it will always be in the way. What you really need is the sort of bag that can be folded or even screwed up and stuffed into a locker somewhere. A holdall that is semi-circular in section, a bit like a Swiss roll with a flat bottom, is particularly useful on a small boat where you may have nowhere to stow your clothes and have to live out of your bag, because it will happily sit on a bunk while you ferret through it to find what you want.

I'm a great believer in wheels because I like to make life easier for myself, so for me a holdall with wheels is the perfect solution. Sometime a big bag is really heavy, even with wheels, in which case consider using two smaller bags with wheels.

However, you must be careful. A friend told me recently of a skipper we both knew who had just bought a new boat which, of course, was his pride and joy. A novice sailor who had recently joined this man's sailing club asked if he could come aboard as crew for a weekend, and the intrepid skipper said yes.

Before the fateful weekend, the skipper sent an e-mail to everyone who was joining him with details of what to bring and what not to bring and was very explicit in asking his crew not to bring bags with wheels, on the grounds that they often get dragged through mud and muck and he didn't want a mess aboard his gleaming new boat, which I thought was very understandable.

Yes, you've guessed it! The new guy turned up, having read and digested the contents of the e-mail, with a holdall on wheels which he immediately lifted off the pontoon and plonked down onto the side deck of the boat, claiming he'd had to ignore the instruction because he had a bad back and couldn't carry a bag by its shoulder strap. What offended the skipper most of all was that the fellow hadn't even phoned or e-mailed him to flag up the problem. He just did his own thing.

This is hardly the behaviour of a team player who willingly accepts the authority of the team captain.

To cut a long story short, by the end of the first day of sailing, during which the man in question exhibited many more examples of narcissistic behaviour, the relationship between him and the skipper had deteriorated to such an extent that he was actually asked to leave the boat, a very drastic step indeed. And most embarrassing for all concerned.

OK, I hear you ask, why do I support the above skipper's decisions when I myself use bags on wheels? The bag is not the point. The answer is that each skipper is different, and he or she each has his own list of do's and don'ts, especially if he or she is also the owner of the boat, and these need to be observed by all concerned.

Let's face it, if you have spent a lot of money on a boat and invited people to join you out of the goodness of your heart, you have a right to lay down the rules. It's that simple. For that reason, always check with the skipper in advance, especially if you feel he's being unreasonable, or if you have any kind of problem in following the skipper's instructions. A discussion with him or her beforehand might reveal the possibility of reaching an amicable solution that meets everyone's needs before things turn nasty.

It's true that bags on wheels can cause damage and bring dirt aboard, so if you do use them, exercise utmost care and awareness. I have to use them simply because I'm not as young as I used to be, but I look where I'm going and make sure I don't roll my bag through anything nasty, I wipe it with a tissue before I take it on board, and once it is on board is has to be carried, not rolled, from one part of the boat to another. If you can't do that, ask someone younger and fitter than you to help.

Another great tip is to use differently coloured plastic carrier bags within your holdall to segregate each type of clothing so you can find it quickly and easily. If you know you need the blue Tesco bag when you want a pair of trousers, or the orange Sainsbury's bag if you want to find a shirt, for example, this helps immensely. And a spare bag for dirty underwear is also a great idea.

This also helps to keep your clothes dry in the event of something leaking onto your bag, and even if you are designated a locker for your clothes it still makes life easier to keep them in their carrier bags within the locker. Moreover, when you go home your waterproof clothing and your towel might still be wet, so it's useful to keep a large spare carrier bag handy to put them in so they don't make everything else in your holdall wet.

That way it's easy to be self-contained. This is especially useful in a small boat where everyone's gear might be thrown into the forepeak or aft cabin, or onto a particular bunk, during the day when everyone wants to go sailing and use the saloon without feeling cluttered.

Nourishment
Over the many years I have sojourned on this beautiful planet of ours it has become abundantly clear to me that each of us is an individual and because of that, our metabolisms differ, so what might be a perfect diet for one person might be complete anathema to another.

For example, I have been told that Sumo wrestlers, who clearly don't worry about trying to lose weight, always eat a huge portion of pasta before a big tournament to give them energy for the forthcoming contest. But if I did that I'd be sluggish, exhausted and overweight in no time.

That's because something in my metabolism, and it took me many years to discover this and work out what to do about it, doesn't work very well in processing carbohydrates to supply whatever the muscles need to produce energy. That means when I eat heavy carbs, especially on a regular basis, I actually have less energy, not more energy. I found out purely by accident that I fare much better on a high protein diet.

For that reason I try to make sure I eat a high protein diet, especially when I'm on a boat, and if I can't get it on the boat I'll make sure I get it when I go ashore. Thus when we were Dutch barging in Holland, in every Friesland village we visited I went ashore and found the local herring shop or stall and made sure to have a plentiful intake of herring (once in my youth I tried vegetarianism for a few months and I thought I was going to die).

Diet is very important because when you go sailing you burn a lot of calories and they need to be replaced with something that will give you plenty of energy, whatever that might be. Therefore it behoves you to find out what it is that suits your particular body and make sure you get plenty of it before, during and after your trip.

We had a friend once who was a vegetarian who didn't like vegetables! Whenever he came on our boat we had to make sure we had a good supply of bread, butter, tomatoes and cheese because all he wanted was cheese and tomato sandwiches, and when we went ashore he sometimes had a crepe or a pizza.

Another of our crew liked fish as long as it didn't look like fish, so it was no use opening a tin of sardines when he was on board, whereas he would consume salmon pate or canned tuna as if it was going out of fashion.

We have another vegetarian friend with whom we were sailing along the coast of Northern Brittany when we pulled into the lovely river at Lezardrieux and went ashore to the local yacht club for a meal. When I told the waitress in my rudimentary French that our friend was a vegetarian she actually look at me as if we had come from another planet and said simply, "what, really?" She was incredulous.

If your preferred eating regime is even just a little unusual, you must tell the skipper, and whoever is going to do the provisioning if it's someone else, exactly what you need to have on board. If I'm invited to sail with a friend I even ask what coffee he has in his galley, and if it's instant I always bring a supply of proper ground coffee, usually my favourite brand, and sometimes the equipment to make a brew, usually a plastic cafetiere. That's because I have a coffee addiction and if I don't get a decent cup of coffee when I get up in the morning I'm not a happy bunny and I might be grumpy all day. What's more if he's stocking up with skimmed or semi-skimmed milk, I'll bring a plastic bottle of full fat milk.

Most important, do let the skipper know if you have any food allergies and obviously avoid those foods like the plague. He won't want you going into anaphylactic shock half way across the English Channel or while zooming through the Alderney race.

Make sure you drink plenty of non-alcoholic drinks. You'd be amazed how quickly a person exposed to the wind and the sun can become dehydrated and you really don't want to let that happen to you. If you don't trust the drinking water on board, make sure there's plenty of bottled mineral water.

Work out from self-observation what you need to give you the required level of energy and nourishment, and make sure it's on board. Food fads can be an endless source of irritation so get it sorted beforehand.

Most important, if you are bringing something you need, bring enough for everyone. I had another friend, a health food fanatic, and he brought his own personal stash of goat's cheese and beetroot, but he secretly kept it in his bag and never offered it to anyone else. This led to a major confrontation with another crew member who found out and, quite justifiably in my opinion, felt hurt that the first guy didn't want to share his precious stuff.

After a little digging I discovered that it was because he simply could not trust there would be enough of his favourite food to last him till the end of the trip. I tactfully suggested to him that when he got home he should take a rest from sailing and seek the services of a really good psychotherapist or counsellor. He was the same chap who frequently turned up in the pub to buy everyone a drink and subsequently found he'd sadly left his wallet on board.

Sailing is not just about sailing skills. It's also about

relationships between people, people who will live together in very close proximity for an allotted time and hope to form bonds of friendship and mutual respect. One person behaving out of alignment with the others can quickly kibosh any such hopes.

Finally, if you need any specific medication, bring that too. But as I said before, never bring illegal drugs on board as this can cause no end of problems for the skipper if they are discovered by the authorities in any country.

Personal hygiene

There are certain things that are best done ashore if you're in a harbour or marina, and that includes going to the toilet and taking a shower, especially if the boat does not have a holding tank to take care of bodily wastes. Most harbours quite rightly do not take kindly towards anyone who discharges raw sewage into their waters. Bear in mind that in some harbours you need to take your own toilet paper with you!

All of the above boils down to common sense and shouldn't need saying really, but unfortunately it also has to be admitted that there are a few people who don't make enough effort over their personal hygiene. This can be a serious problem on a boat. Don't be the person I'm talking about here or there's no way you'll ever be invited back. Even if you have to wash in seawater, make sure you do it frequently.

The same applies to brushing your teeth and shaving, unless you have a beard, in which case keep it tidy and nicely trimmed.

Sleep

You must make sure you get enough sleep and this can be difficult in a boat on passage, otherwise you will soon be sleepy and exhausted, and that's dangerous.

Not only do you greatly increase the risk of having an accident, you might even fall asleep on watch – an unforgivable cardinal sin which can endanger the boat and everyone in it. If everyone is trusting you to keep them safe while they are sleeping, it behoves you to be in good enough physical and mental condition to take care of them.

I've never been able to solve this problem of becoming too tired and in the end I gave up night sailing as it always makes me exhausted.

There was a time when a very good friend who had a boat in Cardiff wanted crew to help him sail her to Torquay, a trip that entailed sailing west along the north coasts of Somerset, Devon and Cornwall, rounding Land's End and then sailing back east along the south coasts of Cornwall and Devon.

For various reasons we decided to do the passage in one go without stopping, and we'd take turns watch-keeping. On the second night I went off watch and retired below to get some shuteye before my next stint which I knew would come around all too soon.

First I tried to sleep in the forepeak but that proved impossible because the boisterous seas kept bouncing me up to the ceiling. The aft cabin was out of the question because the engine was running and it was too noisy in there. That left only the saloon, usually the best place because it's in the vicinity of the fulcrum or pivot point of the boat and is therefore usually the area with the least movement.

The boat was heeling slightly so I climbed onto the leeward bunk and lay down, wondering how I could secure myself from falling on to the floor every time the boat tacked. I tried to wedge myself in and eventually I fell asleep.

Of course the inevitable happened. A rogue wave hit the side of the boat and there was a lurch that launched me into space, still in a horizontal position, and I actually woke up in mid-air. I immediately realised I was going to crash down onto the cabin floor so I instinctively put my arm up to protect my head.

Probably just as well because I did not injure my head. What I did injure when I hit the floor was one of my ribs. In the heat of the moment I hadn't thought of that.

Anyone who has injured a rib will know that it pushes all

the air out of your lungs and it hurts like hell. Trying to breath is also painful. It was a rude awakening to say the least. I just lay on the saloon floor gasping, not wanting to move because I was actually in the safest place. There was nowhere else to fall.

After a few minutes I sat up on the floor against the side of the bunk, taking stock and hoping the pain would soon subside. After ten minutes I staggered to my feet and found some Paracetamol. Then I crawled partly up the companion way steps to inform the skipper, who was on watch with another crew member, of what had happened.

After that any question of sleep for me was completely wiped out with the result that when we finally reached Torquay I was so tired I could hardly stand up or string two words together. I also had a clanging headache and felt thoroughly miserable. For a while I just sat on the cabin bunk staring into space. Then I had to face the challenge of getting home to London, which I did not enjoy one jot.

Moral of the story: If it's your turn to sleep, find somewhere safe where you won't get injured. If necessary sleep on the floor or sleep sitting up on a saloon seat, but whatever you do, make sure you get enough sleep. When I stay overnight on a boat in seriously cold weather, I often wear a woolly hat in bed. It helps me stay warm so I sleep properly. If it's extremely cold I keep some of my clothes on, including my thermal underwear. Anything to get a decent night's sleep!

One caveat – I never take sleeping pills on a boat, just in case of emergency.

One final thing: make sure you have a wristwatch with an alarm, or some such equivalent. If you are taking it in turns to go on watch, it's up to you to be ready on time, even if that means at three o'clock in the morning. And there are many other situations in which you will need to be ready for duty, or to go ashore, or to return on board, at or by a certain time.

Bear in mind, if someone else is waiting to go off watch in the early hours they will feel extremely let down if you are even two minutes late reporting on deck, and it may well be perceived that you are not taking proper responsibility for your duties or caring enough for your fellows.

Eyesight

In the busy and rock-strewn waters around most of our coastlines today, one of our most important physical attributes is effective and efficient eyesight. However, if like me, your vision is not perfect without visual aids, there will soon come a time in your sailing career when you will learn about the limitations of glasses.

I found I was continuously changing between long distance glasses for work on deck, and reading glasses for chart work below, and this became a great source of irritation to me, especially on long passages. I would put my reading glasses "in a safe place" near the chart table only to have to hunt for them in the depths of the bilges as soon as the sea got rough.

As if that wasn't irritating enough, whenever there was spray or rain, my long distance glasses would soon reach a state where I could see better without them, and that was scary!

I tried every oily waxy product known to man and beast, all designed to let the rain or spray drops roll off the lenses in large emulsified dollops, leaving largely clear glass, and I found every one of them as useless as the specially impregnated cloths I also tried. In the end I gave up on using glasses for sailing.

The solution? Contact lenses!

To start with I tried the one day disposables and I could not believe how clearly I could see – far better than with glasses. My optician also gave me a pair of overspecs for reading, but I found I only needed them for the tiniest typematter faintly printed or viewed in very dim light. Mercifully I don't need them for chartwork and tend only to use them in dark Italian restaurants to read the English translation under each dish.

Once I got used to contact lenses, I switched to weekly disposables which are more economical and quite easy to deal with even in a bucking boat. Now when it rains or sprays I simply blink and all is immediately clear again. It's an automatic reflex.

The other great advantage of contact lenses is that you can wear ordinary sunglasses over them. Protecting your eyes from the harmful UV rays of the sun is very important. On a boat you are constantly exposed to the weather and in my books, a decent pair if sunglasses that wrap right round your face is essential, even when the sky is overcast.

I know contact lenses do not suit everyone, but if you are a glasses wearer and you want to go sailing, I would strongly recommend trying them. They have tremendously increased my enjoyment, and I must admit, my competence too. Make sure you give yourself enough time to get used to them before joining the boat.

Finally, a word of warning – if you are going to wear a hat it is well worth investing in one of those small lanyards with a crocodile clip at each end. You can get one in virtually any chandlers for a couple of pounds or so. One end is secured to the hat, the other to your collar.

In the days before I bought one, I used to lose at least five hats per season. Now, thanks to the lanyard, I have had the same hat now for some six or seven seasons. Skippers do not always want to put their boat about just to go fishing for your hat when it blows overboard, especially if the boat is running under spinnaker. In any case, sometimes the hat sinks.

Being organised

It's a very useful to take a small pocket diary in which you can record dates and times of ferry crossings or flights, together with booking references or flight numbers, dates and times for arriving at or departing from the boat, joining details, essential phone numbers and e-mail addresses, and anything else you might require.

If you have been doing shorebased courses to learn yachting, one more thing you might find useful is to bring your course notes with you, and spare paper for making further notes, in a waterproof bag or folder of course. That way, when you get a spare moment, you can look up what you just did to make sure it made sense, and you can look at your notes on anything you might be doing tomorrow so your memory is refreshed in advance. This puts you ahead of the game and helps you understand and learn more quickly.

CHAPTER ELEVEN

MAN OVERBOARD

This is a hotly debated and much chronicled subject which you can read about in all sorts of books on effective skippering, but I have never seen much about it in books addressed specifically to novice crew. And since it is a subject of paramount importance to every person who goes sailing, I decided to include some of the more essential points here, especially with regard to prevention. This is information you need to know.

Everyone on board should concern themselves about man overboard, not just the skipper, for not only is it necessary to know how to cut down the chances of it happening, but the whole ship's company should know what to do if it does happen. It could be your skipper that goes over the side, as very nearly happened to my skipper twice in one afternoon as I described in an earlier chapter, and if you are left on board you need to know how to deal with the situation.

Awareness is your greatest protection against accidents at sea, and maintaining what I call "boat awareness" at all times when on a boat is everybody's responsibility. Caution is another indispensable ally, and when it's rough, extreme caution is even better. A boat is an environment in which it's very easy to have accidents so it's essential to think carefully about every move you make – before you make it! With experience, this will become second nature for most people.

Apart from the obvious danger, a man overboard situation is a complete pain in the backside for everyone left on board, especially the skipper, because not only does the boat have to stop sailing immediately but also it's usually a very difficult and anxiety–provoking exercise to return to someone in the water and then to get them back on board. Obviously prevention is far better than cure, so first of all let's look at some of the ways we can reduce the chances of it happening.

One night in the days when I had my little wooden boat *Lorette*, I was tied alongside another boat which was tied to a pontoon in the middle of the Medina River in the Isle of Wight directly opposite the Folly Inn, a favourite yachty's watering hole. We'd been across to the pub in the little ferry boat where we'd had a great meal and now we were back on board and tucked up in bed. It was about 2.00 a.m.

Suddenly I was awoken from my slumbers by what sounded like someone banging on the hull. I jumped out of my bunk and rushed to the cockpit in my pyjamas where one of my crew who'd been asleep in the saloon also appeared, in his underwear. Then we saw that the skipper of the boat we were tied up to had also run into his cockpit because he'd heard similar banging on his hull. The three of us scanned the water around our boats and suddenly my crew glimpsed a movement out of the corner of his eye.

There was someone in the water and he was being swept by the ebbing tide along the river and although he was trying to grab any low hanging mooring lines he passed, he was unable to get a grip on anything tangible. Instinctively my crew reached down as the man in the water passed between our two cockpits and grabbed his shoulder, or I should say, the shoulder of his waterproof jacket. But the jacket was beginning to slide off him because it wasn't zipped up!

Luckily for him, the other skipper and I managed to get more hands on him and someone got a rope round him, and now we were trying to lift him out of the water, a task that proved impossible because the lifting angle was simply too difficult.

Just then someone else, his friend, came past in a dinghy with only one oar. He was from a vessel moored a few boats up from us and he'd heard the commotion and suspected, quite rightly, that his friend might be in trouble. With his help we managed to manhandle the casualty into the dinghy and then we passed the dinghy's painter hand over hand and boat by boat to the pontoon, where his friend tied the boat up. Finally we clambered over the other boat and onto the pontoon and managed to get the MOB (man overboard) onto that, were he sat dazed, coughing, wheezing and shaking with cold. Someone fetched him a blanket and soon, with his friend's assistance, he was able to stagger back to his boat.

Next morning he came along the pontoon to say thank you. Sheepishly he admitted it had been a case of open fly syndrome, as the Coastguard and the RNLI affectionately call it. Apparently every year people drown from peeing over the side of their boats and falling in, especially after a few drinks at the pub, and when their bodies are found, sure enough, more often than not their flies are open. This man was very lucky because he didn't drown, but undoubtedly he'd come within an ace of doing so.

He told us he'd actually resigned himself to being "a goner" and it was only because he was driven by the tide between our two boats whereupon his self-preservation instinct drove him to bang on our hulls and we acted fast that he survived. That's why I never take sleeping pills when I'm in charge of a boat. You never know when an instant reaction is required.

I tell this story to illustrate how easily a potentially fatal incident can happen on a boat. You can reduce the chances of this happening to you by simply going to the toilet instead of hanging out over the side of your boat for a pee, especially if you've had a few drinks.

I don't mind someone having a couple of drinks when we are safely tied up in harbour, but never enough to lose your awareness and your ability to behave rationally. One of my crew once returned to my boat after he'd had a long session ashore in the pub and he was clearly three sheets to the wind. I refused to let him come back on board until he'd sobered up, so he had to go and find a bed and breakfast for the night. He came back in morning fresh as a daisy and somewhat contrite.

The potential for a MOB is another reason why illegal substances anywhere near a boat are an absolute no no.

Never forget that as crew you are the skipper's responsibility when you are on his boat, and if you become a liability you will not be invited back. Not only is it dangerous, it's antisocial in the extreme, and could cause a lot of problems for the skipper. Apart from that, it's plain bad manners (if your skipper becomes a liability, politely get off the boat at the nearest harbour and go home because it's not safe to sail with him).

On the subject of taking care, I repeat the well worn yachting phrase: "One hand for yourself, one hand for the boat." That means as you move around a moving boat doing jobs on deck or in the cockpit you always hold on to something solid with at least one hand. With every move you make you should be looking for the next handhold. This also will become second nature in time. Caution with awareness must become your default setting, as it were!

Another obvious safety measure you can take at any time is to wear a lifejacket and a harness line, so if you do go over the side you are still attached to the boat. The harness line gives you a huge advantage because it greatly increases the odds of your retrieval, and therefore your survival.

Unlike a buoyancy aid, a lifejacket inflates and a part of it goes behind your neck. That means if you are unfortunate or careless enough to fall in, you will always automatically be turned the right way up, even if you fall in upside down and unconscious. It's obvious that wearing one of these also gives you a huge advantage.

When do you wear a lifejacket? Any time you want. You don't need to wait to be told. And of course, whenever the skipper says so. And when do you wear a harness line? Again, any time you want or when the skipper says so, but NOT if the boat is in danger of sinking or if she's on fire. If she's going down, you do NOT want to be attached!

If you feel seasick, wear a lifejacket and harness. You might be more wobbly than you realise. The same applies if you feel endangered or scared at any time and for any reason.

Nowadays, most lifejackets worth considering have a harness built in, and many have crotch straps which are designed to stop the lifejacket from riding up over your head, which it will try to do as soon as you enter the water. Some also have a hood, which deploys when the lifejacket inflates. You can put this over your face to stop the waves and spray from going into your mouth and up your nose.

The automatic inflation type of lifejacket is the one to go for in my opinion, because you could be unconscious when you hit the water, and therefore unable to find and pull a string to make it inflate.

It's obviously very important to make sure that both the lifejacket and harness are properly buckled up and the strap is correctly adjusted. It's a very good idea for each crew member to try on his or her allocated lifejacket and get it properly adjusted before you set off from the harbour because making the adjustment is a bit of a palaver, and you don't want to be having to do it in a situation of extreme urgency. Even worse, you don't want to have to use it when it's incorrectly adjusted.

When adjusting it bear in mind it has to be loose enough to accommodate not just you, but also maybe a pullover and waterproof jacket, but not so loose that it can float up over your head. In other words, a snug fit is what you are looking for. If crotch straps are provided, I would highly recommend getting over your embarrassment and doing them up. Then, if you do become an unfortunate victim, you have one less thing to worry about.

Once you have done your adjustments, which will almost invariably require the assistance of another crew member, put your lifejacket with your gear in an easily accessible place so you know exactly where it is and can get it in a hurry, and where it won't get mixed up with anybody else's. This then is your lifejacket for the duration of the trip, pre-adjusted and ready to use in an instant. Familiarise yourself with how to put it on and, unless you own it, don't forget to give it back before you go home!

One final point about prevention – if you are feeling queasy, keep away from the sides of the boat and ask someone to fetch the ship's bucket for you.

On the subject of sinking, I once did an RYA Sea Survival course, and what an eye opener that was. Not only did it frighten the life out of me just at the thought of this happening for real, but I was so exhausted at the end of it I climbed into my car and fell asleep for an hour before I felt OK to drive home. It took me a full week to recover.

This led me to understand that if you are overweight (which I was) and/or unfit (which I also was) you have got to do something about it (which I did – please note the use of the past tense) because your life might depend on it.

The Sea Survival course takes place in a swimming pool with a real liferaft, so you can imagine that at sea everything will be ten times more difficult. We were each clad in a swimming costume with our full wet weather gear and an inflated lifejacket over the top. That gear is heavy at the best of times, but if you try to get out of the pool with your pockets full of water, it's like having a ton of bricks round your neck!

The first thing I learned was that trying to swim with all those clothes on is a complete waste of time because the progress you make is so little compared to the effort required, meaning it's of no help at all. Imagine adding a strong wind and tide with waves into the situation and you'll soon realise trying to swim is fruitless unless you can swim in the same direction as the tide. Otherwise the tide will simply take you wherever it wants. Even more serious, you'll soon lose energy and most important, body heat.

In fact, given you are wearing a lifejacket so you will float, the most important thing if you find yourself in the water either as a man overboard or because your boat has sunk, is to preserve your body heat to try to stave off the onset of hypothermia. This you do by floating more or less upright, drawing your knees up under you and clasping your hands together around your knees. If there's more than one of you in the water, it's also a good idea to join hands. That way, a rescuer only has to find one target, and that target is bigger, which makes locating it a little less difficult.

Now of course if someone throws you a lifeline and it's a few yards out of your reach, obviously you will have to swim for it.

Some of the things we practised on the Sea Survival course included stepping or jumping into the liferaft from the side of the swimming pool as if it were the deck of the sinking boat, getting into the raft from the water, helping an unconscious person into the raft, turning it the right way up if it inflates on its side, erecting the awning, deploying the distress signal, and so forth. It was an extremely valuable day and a real wake-up call. Once again you are given indispensable knowledge and also a little experience.

A yacht should have various items of life saving equipment on board and if you value your life and those of your companions, it really is in your best interests to learn how to use them. That's why I would recommend this course, and various others such as First Aid, to anyone who wants to go to sea. You should also learn to use the fire extinguishers, the VHF radio, the bilge pump(s) and any other safety equipment you find on board.

If you do an RYA Competent Crew course, the instructor will no doubt drill everybody in man overboard recovery procedure and for that reason alone it's well worth doing that course as well on the basis that the better prepared you are, the more you will enjoy your sailing and the safer you will be. Getting back to the MOB can be a problem in itself, but an even more difficult one is getting him or her back on board.

There are many different strategies for dealing with such an emergency and the pros and cons of these are often the subject of discussion in the yachting press and Internet forums. No doubt each skipper has a preferred procedure. One thing I would highly recommend is if there are several crew members and someone falls overboard, the first person who sees the incident should yell loudly, "Man Overboard!" and continue to point at the MOB. In fact you must never take your eyes off him and should continue pointing to where he is, especially if the boat is turning and manoeuvring. It's amazing how difficult it can be to find someone in the water, particularly if it's rough or at night. The person pointing should do nothing else and must not allow him or herself to be distracted for an instant until the person in the water has been located and the boat brought back to where he is.

It's also a good idea, if there's a spare crew member, for someone to put out a mayday call on the VHF giving the latitude and longitude co-ordinates of the MOB's last known position. These can be read off from the ship's GPS or if the boat has a DSC radio, the co-ordinates can be read from the display on the VHF. If you are really smart you will hit the MOB button on the GPS system as soon as the MOB is called, to pinpoint the position, and then the GPS can be used to guide the boat back to the MOB. But never rely only on that. Someone should still keep their eyes on him or her.

If you do use the GPS to guide the boat back to the MOB, don't forget to take account of the tide, which will almost certainly have moved him by the time the vessel returns.

At the very least, these measures give you a fighting chance of finding the hapless individual by giving you a reasonable place to start searching. Ideally everyone will know exactly what to do and react so fast the boat never loses sight of him. As a member of the crew, any of these roles and responsibilities could fall on you without warning if you happen to be in the right place at the right time.

Another cardinal rule, always, always, always clip on your harness line at night.

As if locating the man in the water and bringing the boat back to him was not problem enough, now comes the task of getting him back on board, and this can be a real brain teaser. Opinions are as divided on this as in most problems in boating.

The first thing to bear in mind is that you will probably have dropped the sails and put the engine on by the time you return to the MOB, therefore you must be extremely mindful of not letting your propeller go anywhere near him. This can be extremely dangerous. As soon as you come within range the safest thing to do is to not only put the gear control in neutral, but actually stop the engine so that the gearbox, and thus the propeller, cannot be accidentally re-engaged by someone falling on the throttle control. Try to position the boat so the MOB is to leeward and therefore getting some shelter from the boat.

The most basic piece of equipment to get some back on board is the boarding ladder. I have one permanently mounted on the transom of my boat which folds down so the lowest rungs are well below the waterline. If the man is conscious and able to reach the stern, he should be able to climb the ladder to get back aboard, perhaps with assistance from above. Simple, one would have thought!

Of course even this simple solution has its problems, the biggest of which is that if someone in the water approaches the stern of your boat, you cannot under any circumstances use your propeller. If the person can reach the ladder on his own, so be it, but usually the only solution is to come near him more or less amidships, stop the engine and throw him a floating line, which he has to tie round his middle.

Then someone on the boat should be able to gently and carefully walk him round to the stern using the floating line.

Also be aware that in a rough sea the boat's transom will almost certainly be bouncing up and down and there is a considerable danger to someone in the water approaching the rear of the boat being hit on the head by the stern of the boat and rendered unconscious or perhaps even killed or brain-injured.

If for any reason the boarding ladder idea won't work or is deemed to be too dangerous, and because I am well aware that even Tarzan would find that heaving a person aboard a rocking yacht is well nigh impossible, I have various lifting devices on my boat. The most basic of these is a Life Sling.

This is simply a long floating line with a floating harness on the end of it. The other end must be permanently attached to the boat. The idea is you drive the boat slowly around the MOB in a wide arc while letting the Life Sling stream from the stern. As long as the radius of the boat's circle is less than the length of the floating line, at some point the line must meet the path of the MOB, at which time he grabs it, you stop the boat, and wait while the MOB fastens the harness around his waist. Then someone on board gently pulls him towards the boat.

If the MOB is capable of using the boarding ladder, then simply pull him around to the stern, checking first of course that there is no chance of the propeller suddenly starting up or the transom hitting his head. If that won't work, it's time to deploy the lifting tackle, which every well-equipped yacht should have on board.

I also have another very clever device called a Tri Buckle. It's simply a triangular piece of strong, porous fabric that can sink which, to summarise briefly, enables the MOB to be more or less rolled horizontally up the side of the hull and into the boat under the guard rail, with the aid of the aforementioned six to one purchase lifting tackle. An undignified way to report back on board but if it works, hey, who cares about that?

Finally, if you or any of your colleagues have the misfortune of getting a dunking, be aware of the danger of hypothermia, which I am given to understand, kills more people than drowning!

Someone recovering from hypothermia must be warmed up slowly and never given alcohol because that can cause further body heat loss. Probably it's best to put them below decks in some dry clothing, perhaps in bed, and give them a warm, sweet cup of tea (unless they are hypoglycaemic or diabetic). One of those silver foil-type survival blankets wrapped around the victim is ideal. And someone must keep an eye on the person at all times. Be prepared to make a mayday call at once if the victim looks to be getting worse. I emphasise, if anyone's life is in imminent danger for whatever reason, do not hesitate to send a mayday call, however inexperienced you might be.

If it's serious but it doesn't look as if the victim will die, be prepared to send a Pan Pan Medico distress call on the VHF, especially if you need urgent medical advice. In serious cases the authorities might even send a helicopter to put a paramedic on board, or to lift the person off and whisk them to hospital. In an extreme situation, you might be able to call a helicopter to lift the MOB straight out of the sea.

You do yourself a huge favour if you also do the RYA course that teaches you how to use a VHF radio. This will earn you a VHF Radio Operator's Licence which gives you the authority (and knowledge) to operate the radio without supervision. Only too often the only person qualified, and therefore authorised, to use this equipment is the skipper, and you might be the one trying to get him rescued or hospitalised.

Of course, in an extreme situation you would not hesitate to try using it whether you are licensed or not.

Finally, please understand this chapter is in no way a comprehensive treatment of this subject. The aim is to give you enough information to impress upon you the importance of this matter and to encourage you to go more deeply into it yourself. Forewarned is forearmed, as the saying goes, and you can't put a price on knowledge, especially in an emergency.

My faithful mantra applies just as much to this topic as to any other sailing matter: "The better you and your boat are prepared, the more trouble-free your sailing will be."

CHAPTER TWELVE

SUPPORT YOUR LONELY SKIPPER

A boat is for life, not just for Christmas.

All conscientious skippers are keenly aware of the awesome responsibility that looking after their vessel entails. Every springtime the necessity rears its ugly head for expensive, backbreaking and endless maintenance if the longevity of their pride and joy is to be assured. And at the end of every autumn, there's the sad and soulless job of laying up. Laying up symbolises the end of an all too brief sailing season, and it means more back-breaking work.

Most club skippers do not expect any financial input towards maintenance from crew members, but donating your man (or woman) power, preferably unstintingly, is always well received. One man on his own can prepare and antifoul a 32 foot yacht with one coat in a morning with the aid of a roller, but with your help you could both be finished and relaxing in the pub by elevenses' time.

Skippering, or more specifically boat owning, can be a long and lonesome road to travel and skippers are actually human – they like to feel supported and they hate feeling they are taken for granted. If you are only in it for the good times you miss half the game. So don't disappear at fitting-out time, especially if you have a vital skill such as painting or making tea. After all, the skipper is shelling out shedloads of dosh and out of his sheer good nature you're getting a virtually free ride, so the least you can do is to help him when there's only work to do and no sailing.

I write this chapter on board my boat in France and I've just finished the backache-inducing and knuckle grazing job of servicing the engine in readiness for the forthcoming season. And guess what? I'm doing it on my own, so I'm really feeling this.

Show your skipper you care. A new chart or fender is always a welcome Christmas present (you can't have too many fenders).

Winter is also a good time to learn some theory, or even something practical that is sailing related but shore based. Only this February I did a one day course in Marine Electronics in a freezing cold classroom in Southampton and a week later for the second time I did the one day RYA Engine Maintenance course in the same classroom though this time it was even colder – in fact it snowed briefly. Luckily for the second of the courses I wore a warmer pullover.

Now if you did a course like that, you could come and help me next year and you'd be in my good books forever! If only I could persuade my crew to go on such courses I'd be absolutely blissed out!

As I have said many times before, there's no substitute for knowledge, and sailing courses give you the kind of knowledge that's easy to acquire. You just pitch up to a classroom and the information is virtually handed to you on a plate. You may write a few notes and you have to pay attention, and you may have to do some homework exercises, but that's all.

The other thing for which there is no substitute is experience and that's not so easy. You can't get experience just by throwing money at it, you have to put in the time and the hard yards. By doing what you can to educate yourself you are much more likely, when the sailing season gets going, to get invited on board repeatedly, and then you will begin to acquire experience.

And what a fantastic thing to learn – the art of helping to conduct a boat under sail from A to B safely. Show your commitment, do a training. Your skipper will appreciate it.

If I were asked to recommend which courses a novice crew should consider doing as basic, I would suggest the following:

♠ Competent Crew

♠ First Aid

♠ Sea Survival

♠ Engine Maintenance

♠ VHF Radio Operator

All of the above are available through RYA approved training establishments, and details of the courses can be found on the RYA website (in case you are wondering, I have no vested interest in recommending RYA courses, save for trying to raise crewing standards). Most skippers will welcome you with open arms if you take the trouble to do even just one of these courses.

This is a cleat.
OK, enough about the winter. Your real purpose as crew, apart from adding to the social side of things, is to support your skipper as I said, so while we're on the subject of how you can do that let's look now at some other ways you could be a real help while afloat.

The first things I teach a novice when he or she comes aboard is, "this is a cleat, this is a warp and this is a fender, and this is what we do with them." When the skipper is instructing you in the basic drill for mooring up or casting off, pay particular attention, for it is one of the most important things you will have to do for him, apart from taking the helm while he goes to the toilet. As you will soon find out, mooring up and casting off have a great propensity for going pear-shaped, especially when there are lots of bystanders watching, so it helps if you become good at it.

Every skipper has his own style (some would say foibles) or preferences about how he or she wants things done, so don't argue. For many jobs on a boat either there is no "right way", or there are several ways, all equally "right". In many cases there is also the definitive "RYA method", and some techniques work better on one boat whereas a different method might be better suited to another boat. Unless you know the boat and skipper well, the only thing you can do is to assume the skipper knows his boat and what's best for her.

On my boat there is only "what works". That means, this way works for me on this boat, and that is the way I want it done! A skipper's sense of security is of paramount importance to him or her and if he has a way of doing something he can depend on because he knows from experience it will work, then you are expected to comply. Never forget, a boat is neither a democracy nor a debating chamber.

For example, one hard and fast rule of mine is never to do a locking turn on a halyard or a sheet, and only on a mooring line if absolutely necessary. Another one that I mentioned before is, when critical manoeuvres, such as leaving or approaching harbour or setting or lowering sails, are about to take place all mobile phones are to be switched off or switched to silent, including mine.

Other excellent skippers may have shown you different ways of doing the job in question, and they may be perfectly valid. But if your present skipper wants it done differently, do it his way. Unless he is incompetent or inexperienced, his way will almost certainly be just as effective as any other way. If you are still convinced the other skipper's way was better, do it the way you have been asked this time and later, when everyone is in relaxed mode, very tactfully and sensitively discuss and compare the two ways with the present skipper. Or even better, phone him at home afterwards when he's alone and can talk in private without feeling embarrassed or challenged.

This is of paramount importance, for there is nothing calculated to irritate a skipper more than being contradicted or argued with by a crew member, especially in a crisis or in the middle of a critical manoeuvre, and even more so when others are present. At such times, and particularly in an emergency, there is no time for discussion.

Never forget, whatever happens on a boat is the skipper's responsibility, so if a manoeuvre goes wrong after you have done precisely what has been asked of you, you can't be blamed. Skippers are by default very independent free spirits and they like to make their own mistakes and learn their own lessons – if necessary, the hard way.

One more plea from this hard pressed skipper – when the skipper is briefing his crew about an upcoming manoeuvre, please listen carefully and pay attention, even if he is teaching his grandma to suck eggs. Make sure you understand exactly what he wants you to do and when. If necessary politely seek clarification or confirmation of any point in his instructions, no matter how subtle or nitpicking it may seem.

The only exception: If you have exceptionally good grounds for doubting the skipper's competence and are seriously concerned he is about to do something that could put the ship in danger, then of course I would expect you to respectfully point out the problem you think you have identified and diplomatically suggest an alternative course of action.

Be careful though. Incompetent skippers tend to have even more delicate egos than ones who know exactly what they are doing, and if the skipper gets one whiff that he feels he's under attack, he will almost certainly become defensive, and then it will be virtually impossible to get through to him. All you need in such a case is for one thing to go wrong and he'll be badmouthing you all round the yacht club when you come ashore which, needless to say, won't do much for your campaign to be invited crewing more often. Whatever you do, never undermine your skipper.

Now to round off this chapter, here are a couple of really silly stories that illustrate the kind of thing that results in skippers tearing their hair out. Don't let the real life characters in these stories be you!

A long time ago a group of friends charted a boat for a weekend of fun around the Solent. When they were returning the boat to base they decided to refuel before giving the boat back to the charter company, and when the boat reached the fuelling berth one crew member who shall remain nameless to spare his blushes, was given the job of refuelling the boat and refilling the water tanks.

Yes, you've guessed it! Because he wasn't thinking properly about what he was doing, he filled the diesel tank with water and the water tank with diesel, a hugely embarrassing mistake and a costly one to boot.

Now here's an interesting question: in a case like that, who should foot the inevitable bill? It seems unfair that the whole crew should chip in for one person's idiotic mistake, and it also seems unfair that the skipper should have to pay, although you could argue that the person in question should have been comprehensively briefed on the task and/or carefully supervised by someone who knew what was what. Should the culprit cough up, or is it unreasonable to expect a moderately inexperienced person to get it right without instruction? I don't know how the matter was resolved, but hey, filling a fuel tank with fuel and a water tank with water is not rocket science. This is what I mean when I say skippers expect crew members to exercise their common sense and powers of observation, and if they are not sure, to ask before it's too late. On every boat I have ever been on the word "FUEL" is clearly embossed on the cap of the fuel tank inlet, and the word "WATER" on the water inlet cap.

Perhaps the insurance paid?

The other silly story concerns the same person, believe it or not. This time a group of friends from the same yacht club chartered a boat for another trip and off they went into the wild blue yonder. When they returned to base the skipper asked this same fellow to take down the club burgee (small flag) they had been flying from the starboard spreader, which he did with great alacrity.

The only problem was he also brought down the halyard with it. In this context the halyard is a thin but strong length of line used to hoist and lower a burgee or courtesy flag which is left permanently rigged through a fitting on the spreader as in effect a continuous loop of rope. Now to get it back through the fitting on the spreader, someone would have to be hoisted part way up the mast. Not as serious or costly as the misdemeanour in the first story but nonetheless irritating and embarrassing for the skipper and due to pure thoughtlessness.

A skipper already has to deal with enough problems even when things are going well, and anything you do to add to them will not do you any favour. He wants your support. He wants you to be dependable. He wants you to be firing on all four cylinders. So beware. Use your noddle and make it your business to be aware!

CHAPTER THIRTEEN

SOME FINAL THOUGHTS AND TIPS

When, as a novice, you step on board someone's yacht, the skipper should give you a comprehensive safety briefing, but let's face it, often they don't for one reason or another. If that happens and you are a relative novice, ask him for one. You never know, it might save your life.

- ♠ Always think safety. One hand for the boat and one hand for yourself!

- ♠ Make sure you know the use and importance of lifejackets and harnesses, fire extinguishers and fire blanket, escape hatches, flares, VHF, liferaft, MOB, the bilge pump(s), and all matters safety.

- ♠ Get your lifejacket adjusted before you set off and practise putting it on. You never know when you might need it in a hurry.

- ♠ Don't be embarrassed to ask how the toilet should be used and make sure you understand what to do about any sea cocks that might be involved.

- ♠ If there's anything you don't understand, ask, don't guess – it could be a safety issue.

- ♠ Remember, no skipper in his right mind will expect a novice to have any sailing skills or knowledge. What he will expect is for you to take responsibility for your own wellbeing (eg, put on that pullover before you get cold), not to leave your gear lying around in a mess (have consideration for your fellow sailors), display a genuine eagerness to learn and to pitch in when things need to be done, not to shy away from the washing up when it's your turn, to be prepared to pay your share of day-to-day expenses without complaint, and to use your common sense and intelligence at all times. In other words, all the stuff you do at home that you don't need to learn in a sailing school.

♠ Observe all social etiquette – don't drink to excess, don't smoke on a non-smoking boat, never bring animals or illegal drugs on board, and certainly never bring weapons, explosives or highly flammable substances. Always be considerate to the others, even if you hate them. Don't embarrass your skipper. If you have to cross another boat to get ashore, always walk round the bow rather than the stern, unless that's impossible.

♠ If you're going abroad, always bring an up-to-date passport, some foreign currency as well as emergency money and a credit card.

♠ Make sure you are covered by insurance, particularly medical insurance, and especially when going abroad, and get any relevant inoculations well in advance.

♠ Make sure you bring with you a really warm sleeping bag.

♠ Always bring suitable clothing appropriate to the climate where you'll be sailing and don't forget even places like the Caribbean can get chilly in the evening.

♠ Above all, be aware – of what's going on around you, of what's going on within you, and with due regard to all matters of safety and caution.

♠ The London and Southampton Boat Shows, and lots of other boat shows around the country and abroad, can be a lot of fun and they are great places to meet people in the world of boating, the sailing schools, the charter companies, boat and equipment dealers and of course the RYA.

- If you're a fashionista there's plenty of scope for you in the world of boating, and not only for women, as you will see at the nautical clothing outlets. But be warned, you'd better have deep pockets.

- It's great to immerse yourself in the world of boating and to feel energised, even inspired, by meeting like-minded people, especially in the type of boating you are attracted to. For example, if you love classic boats, especially wooden ones, there's no better place to visit than the Festival of the Sea held in Brest every four years. It's truly a huge spectacle, and you never know, someone might need a crew at the last minute when they go out on the water, in which case you actually become an exhibit, or part of one, because literally thousands of people will be watching your every move from the shore and from other boats. There are lots of smaller classic boat festivals all over the place and they all feature great food, drink and music as well as fascinating boats.

- Oh yes, I almost forgot: don't obsess about the more serious matters I've raised. Take them seriously, of course, but never lose sight of the idea that the most important thing is to enjoy yourself, otherwise it's a pointless exercise!

- Don't drive your skipper bonkers.

Here's one final ridiculous story that illustrates just how obsessive compulsive a skipper can be (I'm sorry to say I'm talking about myself).

This story concerns a friend of mine who came sailing with his wife with me and my wife on our new boat, of course our pride and joy. The character in this story will know who he is so if you're reading this my friend, I hope you won't take it amiss. I simply must tell this story because it so poignantly illustrates how ridiculously over sensitive a skipper can be.

In the galley we have a magnetic knife rack above the sink on which I have stowed all our kitchen knives and scissors.

It so happened purely by chance that I had placed them all with their handles upwards. I don't know why.

After a couple of days of sailing together my friend remarked that he thought it was dangerous to have the knives that way up because if one fell off the rack while someone was working at the sink, the point of the blade, which would be facing downward, could go into the person's hand.

I told him I couldn't see the danger and that I was perfectly happy with my arrangement and I had no intention of turning the knives the other way up.

Blow me down when I returned to the boat from a stroll ashore the next day, I noticed that all the knives on the rack had been turned around so the handles were now pointing down! I couldn't believe my eyes and I had to do a double take.

As if that wasn't enough, later I noticed that all the cutlery in the drawer had been turned around as well. This was too much! I declared war while he was ashore and turned everything back round to the way I had it before. It felt like a coup or a mutiny designed to undermine the King or the President of this tiny floating kingdom, or to usurp his authority at the very least.

He must have got the point because although nothing was said it didn't happen again. Sometimes actions speak louder than words and I have a feeling he could sense my smouldering anger at the cheek of it. To come on someone else's boat and rearrange things when he had been expressly told by the skipper that he didn't want them to be rearranged!

So who's being obsessive compulsive, me or him? Sometimes it's hard to tell. The point as far as I'm concerned was not so much what he did, but that he did it on the quiet while I was away from the boat and against my wishes!

I've found this happens from time to time – someone does something to undermine my authority while I'm away from the boat because they have an obsession.

There's no getting away from it, skippers are control freaks and they have no intention of changing that condition. If you can't fit in with that ethos then either give up sailing or get your own boat and become a skipper yourself.

***

At the start of the first chapter I reported how so many of the skippers I meet just can't find the crew they need, and that those who do get invited back often are members of a tiny elite. I hope now, if you have read this book, that you can understand why, and what you have to do to join that elite. As I say, it's all about attitude, attitude, attitude.

Good luck and great sailing!

ABOUT DAVE ROBSON

Dave Robson's writings are about being the best you, and what he says can be applied in any field, not just sailing.

Dave took up sailing after his divorce in 1984. Since then he's owned a variety of boats starting with a Mirror dinghy. His current pride and joy is *Prana,* a Contest 40s yacht he keeps in France.

Apart from having skippered his own and various charter boats numerous times, many and varied are the yachts he's crewed on over the years, sailing with a variety of skippers. When he started he knew nothing about sailing nor did he know anyone with a boat, so he completed every RYA yacht training course and exam from Competent Crew to Yachtmaster Offshore and Yachtmaster Ocean Theory. He is also a qualified shorebased instructor.

Along the way, Dave has accumulated many colourful stories and experiences with which to illustrate the points he makes in this book and has been invited back to crew many times on the boats of his sailing companions.

Dave has had many careers, starting in advertising (which he hated), moving on to journalism (which he loved), followed by a fourteen year spell working as a carpenter. After that he decided to follow his deep interest in personal development by training and then working for some thirteen years as a life coach. Now Dave is a full time author whose first loves are writing and sailing.

Dave's first book, *The Five Pillars of Happiness,* about personal transformation and how to engineer your life to make it exactly as you want it to be, is available directly from Wizard Publishing, or on-line.

Dave also has a free monthly e-newsletter, *Namaste,* for people who want to live more consciously, and a blog, *Heavenly Vibrations,* also focused on conscious living, which he updates whenever he can find time between writing books, articles and *Namaste.*

You can read more about Dave's work by visiting *www.dave-robson.com*